13 Principles to Power Your Life Forward

by Stephen Jacques

Copyright © 2025 by Stephen Jacques

All rights reserved. No part of this publication may be reproduced, distributed, or transmitted in any form or by any means, including photocopying, recording, or other electronic or mechanical methods, without the prior written permission of the publisher, except in the case of brief quotations embodied in critical reviews and certain other noncommercial uses permitted by copyright law.

ISBN: 979-8-9987882-0-8

13 Principles to Power Your Life Forward

Stephen Jacques

Bold moves, or nothing happens.

—Keith Richards

CONTENTS

FOREWORD 1

1 **PURSUE YOUR PASSIONS** 7
   - Identifying Your Passions

2 **BUILD PERSEVERANCE AND CONFIDENCE** 23
   - Developing a Winning Attitude
   - Surrounding Yourself with the Right People

3 **COMMIT TO HONESTY AND AUTHENTICITY** 37
   - Committing to Honesty and Authenticity
   - Maintaining Momentum

4 **OVERCOME PROCRASTINATION AND MENTAL BARRIERS** 47
   - Overcoming Procrastination
   - Digging Deep into the Unknown
   - Analyzing Personality Types

5 **TAKE RESPONSIBILITY** 59
   - Avoiding Self-Pity
   - Breaking Mental Barriers
   - Challenging Yourself

6 **ADDRESS SELF-SABOTAGE** 75
   - Addressing Deep-Seated Thoughts and Feelings
   - Overcoming Self-Sabotage
   - Flexibility for Change

7 **DEFINE AND ACHIEVE SUCCESS** 87
   - Defining Success
   - Prioritizing Personal Goals
   - Avoiding Comparisons

8   MANAGE TIME EFFECTIVELY 99
- Judicious Time Management
- Avoiding Negative Influences
- Disengaging from Social Media

9   CLEAR OUT NEGATIVITY 109
- Resetting and Starting Fresh
- Streamlining Operations
- Avoiding Unsatisfactory Partnerships

10   NAVIGATE FAMILY AND SOCIAL PRESSURES 121
- Dealing with Opinions of Family Members
- Blazing Your Own Trail

11   NETWORK AND LEARN 127
- Networking Strategies
- Learning From Industry Leaders

12   DEVELOP RESILIENCE 137
- Handling Setbacks
- Developing Resilience

13   IMPLEMENT DAILY SUCCESS STRATEGIES 149
- Daily Strategies for Success
- Taking Life One Day at a Time

LET THINGS FLOW 161
CONCLUSION 165
A FINAL THOUGHT 169
ACKNOWLEDGMENTS 171
ABOUT THE AUTHOR 173

FOREWORD

Nothing BIG ever came from being SMALL.

This book of positivity and optimism exists to help you identify your passions and cultivate the perseverance, balance, and confidence to create a life more fulfilling and purposeful than you ever imagined. The goal is to shape a meaningful existence—one that channels your highest aspirations, dedication, grit, and love—sending a powerful force of good karma into the world.

Confidence grows through trying—action—it is not something you sip from a soda can.

You absolutely deserve happiness. It's not just a wish—it's a choice. Every day, you decide whether to embrace a positive mindset or allow negativity to take hold. Like sadness, happiness is something we consciously or unconsciously choose. Be a doer and *start*. Confidence is built through persistence—crafted through effort and repetition, not big talk.

You are unstoppable when you have the power to push beyond the comfort zone. Boasting a motivated mind, empowering principles, and a winner's mindset; to conquer the fight within and live fearlessly. Armed with the right skills, and polishing them, you'll confidently address whatever comes your way; becoming a mighty force. What you focus on—and the state of your mind—becomes you. It directs your actions. Behavior and daily habits emerge from our mindset.

Your imagination knows no bounds and can take you places beyond your wildest dreams. Complacency lurks in the shadows, but the power to choose your path has always been yours. Life rewards steady progress—moving with purpose and flowing with the natural rhythm of things rather than forcing them. Slow and steady indeed wins the race. This applies whether you're launching a new project, navigating relationships, or persevering through obstacles. Your power is to choose what you think about, through which lens, and when to execute.

Do you believe in fate or destiny, or do you think incredible outcomes are simply the result of sheer—or perhaps dumb—luck? Are you open to change, or do you see yourself as stubborn? What perspective shapes the way you view the world, because of that, are you currently *stuck*?

Every day, we face a choice: to see ourselves as victims of life's challenges or to rise as confident, patient leaders. In the past month, how many people have you genuinely lifted up or inspired? How often have you told someone, "You're going to have a great life—I can just feel it"? Empowering others not only strengthens them but also reveals the areas where we need to grow ourselves. Will this journey be solely about your personal success, or will it also be about uplifting others? The energy you put into the world—through kindness, encouragement, and generosity—returns to you in powerful ways. If you haven't been able to uplift others, we'll uncover why—digging into self-talk, self-awareness, and the barriers preventing you from becoming the best version of yourself.

This approach isn't just fulfilling—it's the foundation of real success and gives your life *meaning*. There's something remarkable about people who, despite humble beginnings, are fearless, resourceful, and unshakably strong. It's no coincidence that success tends to follow them. When faced with challenges, they dig deep, tapping into a well of resilience they didn't even know they had. These individuals don't wait for opportunities; they create them—and in doing so and simply trying—they bring their wildest dreams to life.

The fulfillment that comes from overcoming obstacles is immeasurable. Inaction almost always leads to predictable disappointment, while those who put in the effort—who truly earn their success—gain a deeper sense of purpose and lasting value. Seeking advice from those who have *walked the path and succeeded* is far wiser than listening to those who merely speculate about what might happen. This is extremely important to embrace—saving time and money.

My family didn't have it easy—nothing was handed to us. We had to rely on self-motivation: work hard or be left behind. Looking back, I realize this was one of the greatest gifts we could have received. Whether it was pursuing education or figuring out life, we had to make it work on our own, with little to no support. Complaining or blaming others was never an option. My Italian and French grandparents, who lived through the Great Depression, would have been baffled by complaints. For them, grit was the foundation of success. We adopted that same mindset early on, pushing forward aggressively, efficiently, and without excuses. Hard work, character, integrity, and selflessness became our way of life.

I once had a colleague ask me 25 years ago, "I know you're doing [such and such], but is that tapping into the real *you in you*?" That question stuck with me. Are you engaging in something that aligns with your deepest passions and who you truly are at your core? Or are you merely settling for what seems good enough?

A college friend of mine once hosted a TV interview show, and I asked him how he conducted his interviews so smoothly. Wasn't it challenging?

He said, "I'm talking to them about their favorite subject." I responded, "Yeah? What's that?"

He smiled slyly. "Themselves."

Growing up in Richmond, Virginia, in the seventies shaped me. It was a time of simple, solid, down-to-earth people. I have vivid memories of walking to the pool on hot summer days, exploring the woods, riding motorcycles down dusty trails, and swimming in the *rapids* of the James River. These experiences formed the foundation of who I am, cultivating lifelong friendships built on trust and authenticity. Even today, I know those friends would be there for me, genuinely and without pretense. Public schools offered sports, clubs, and a strong sense of community. The city's Fan District was alive with music, culture, and creativity. We were content and didn't know any different. It wasn't about what you had—it was about who you were as a person.

After 40 years of navigating technical and artistic careers, experiencing highs and lows, and crossing paths with incredible individuals, I felt compelled to share the motivational insights in this book. Some moments and lessons stuck with me, like when a colleague said, "It's easier to stay in a rut than it is to get out of one." That statement hit me hard. Millions are *stuck*.

As you read through this book, I'll challenge you with open-ended questions, encouraging you to reflect on your passions and specific purpose. These prompts are meant to ignite something inside you—to spark a fire that pushes you to take action, set goals, and create a life that makes you feel proud and fulfilled. Yes, the details can be overwhelming but avoid procrastination. No one else can define your intentions and purpose—you must do that for yourself.

When you commit to making things happen—despite obstacles—you cultivate not just success, but true fulfillment. This is your power. Your attitude and mindset are your steering wheel and gas pedal, while good health and a positive outlook serve as the engine that keeps you moving forward. Take control, and navigate toward a future filled with meaning, purpose, and self-realization. Each day, remind yourself of two simple yet most powerful letters: OP—*Other People*. When you prioritize others ahead of yourself, you'll gradually see your life shift into a more fulfilling, unselfish, and deeply rewarding space. Listen closely to them, you will love it.

Now, let's dig deep and uncover the authentic *you in you*. Critics, distractions, jealousy, comparisons, and naysayers will always be there, trying to drain your energy and slow you down—if you let them. But remember this: the only person who has ever truly told you that you couldn't do something is *you*. When we lie to ourselves, we waste time and do ourselves a disservice.

Take a moment to reflect on that. Your daily self-talk not only shapes your direction but also defines the limits of your imagination. With discernment and maturity, you'll learn to cut through the noise—building the most effective principles and habits that will propel your life forward.

It's interesting that when others make mistakes, it's easy to quickly assign negative labels and blame. But when we make mistakes, we rationalize, vehemently defend ourselves—excuses quickly arise. For souls who wholly disappoint or possibly awful individuals you've dealt with, can steal your joy; I ask you this: You don't like what they did, so it stopped your joy. This logic doesn't make sense, does it? Derailed from their behavior—will be addressed.

This isn't a "fake it 'til you make it" kind of book, nor is it filled with shallow advice. Nor tricking your mind into thinking it is something it truly is not. My hope is that you'll find the *real deal*—the genuine, the authentic—the opposite of surface-level success. Like the difference between a true artist and a manufactured celebrity. I hope these pages offer insights that guide you along your journey—a foundation to launch. Knowing yourself and building confidence will be on this ride.

Best,

Stephen Jacques

1
PURSUE YOUR PASSIONS

The journey to fulfillment begins with self-reflection. Identify moments when you felt genuinely happy and analyze the activities and environments that contributed to those feelings. Ask yourself questions to uncover your passions and plan how to integrate them into your life.

THIS CHAPTER COVERS:

Identifying Your Passions
- *Reflect on past experiences to discover what brings you joy.*
- *List activities that make you feel alive and fulfilled.*
- *Narrow down your choices and embark on your new path.*

IDENTIFYING YOUR PASSIONS

Reflect on Past Experiences to Discover What Brings You Joy

The euphoria of spending your life pursuing your true passions may seem like an impossible dream, a reality reserved for the rare and lucky. But dreams are the fuel that drives us to greatness—they give us the courage to take risks, the resilience to overcome obstacles, and the ingenuity to find new paths to reach our goals.

Creating an amazing life with true meaning and purpose may seem daunting, particularly if you've built a life of routine and stability and have many responsibilities to others. For some, even identifying a true passion may seem overwhelming, if not impossible. Cast those negative thoughts aside. With sufficient soul-searching, followed by deliberate planning, you can find the true you in you: the core where your dreams and goals reside, possibly buried under years of responsibility and drudgery that so many assume is simply the way life is.

Happiness doesn't require accumulating material things; it's about being present and nourishing your soul with what truly matters. While some areas of your life may already bring fulfillment, it's essential to continue exploring new avenues for growth. This collection of thoughts aims to inspire self-motivation in every area of your life, help you break free from feeling stuck or stifled, and guide you to prosperity through the development of your unique skills and talents.

Begin by absorbing and researching the things you MOST love. Remember that an open mind can operate only after you've eradicated any long-held insecurities or doubts you may harbor. There are many options, but there's no need to plug yourself into a random effort. Be specific in each move you make. Don't waste time unless things feel right—trust your gut instinct, that feeling deep in your soul. If you need to hire a life coach or someone similar to help you set a direction, give it a try. Book a one-hour session for a quick chat of discovery; you'll most likely be glad you did.

Take breaks along the way—don't burn out in the process of searching. Exciting opportunities often arise in the least-expected places; sometimes, they've been staring you in the face all along, unbeknownst to you.

At the end of the day, if you're the type of person who prefers a simple, practical life—a stable, safe, and predictable job—try that option. If a job with the government or a large company seems like your cup of tea, give it a spin. You're not committed forever, but no one knows better than you whether it's the right fit. Don't do yourself a disservice by accepting something that's a poor match. Give these decisions a lot of thought, pressing down hard on your highest priorities. Write them down and rank them via pros and cons.

To do this, you need information. The more questions you ask others, the more you'll find your personal groove and a defined direction. Before you accept any position or step into something significant, take the time to get to know the staff. How does their attitude and spirit feel to you? What is the condition of the space you may be working in? Why not attend a luncheon or company gathering to immerse yourself in the company culture and its dynamics? Get to know the vibe as much as you can, as if you were already an employee. Consider vacation schedules and how much time you'd spend away from loved ones.

Fully dig into all the details, understanding the varied responsibilities and exactly what you're about to undertake. This will let you develop a mental list on how to proceed—gleaned and culled from the subjects we'll touch upon in the chapters ahead.

While studying engineering, a family friend gave me a Summer construction job. Amidst Virginia's scorching heat, he caught me off-guard one day by saying, "Do something big so I can brag about you". He didn't mean it in a boastful, egotistical way. What he meant was: go challenge yourself, set ambitious goals, aim for greatness in whatever you do, and, above all, give it everything you've got. Why not defy mediocrity and complacency? Life is short, and we only get one shot. Don't waste it. Push yourself. Give your best, leave no stone unturned, and approach everything with intensity—because, why not? I was exhausted after those 5 college years, yet character was built, endless lessons were learned. It makes us fearless, courageous, confident.

A friend once shared his ideal employee profile for his law team: "Give me a leader—president of a fraternity, bandleader, captain of the baseball team, head fundraiser for St. Jude's or a cancer center." The message? Leadership shapes people in extraordinary ways. When you step up to lead, something magical happens—your confidence grows, your ability to work with others comes alive, and the team concept takes hold. After all, few significant achievements are accomplished alone—there's always someone involved, in some way, big or small.

That same man, with his big smile and candid demeanor, once told me when I asked his opinion about someone I had just met, "Hey, I like everybody." It wasn't just a simple response—it reflected his mindset: always taking the higher road, always choosing the positive path, and succeeding because of it. In his spare time, he raised over one hundred million dollars for St. Jude's Children's hospital founder and friend Danny Thomas.

"Isn't that great.... ain't you somethin'?" was his response to almost everything—a mindset that shaped his entire *being*. If that positive mantra played as an incantation in your mind, if it became your default, how in the world could you lose? Let's say you noted a divorce to someone like him, for example, they may think or say, *"It's amazing how you're soon going to be with the person you were truly meant to be with."* Or, *"just remember how much your family and I both love you".* No matter the situation, these souls refuse to see anything but the bright side. Relentless positivity isn't just self-talk—it radiates in conversations, especially when surrounded by other successful, like-minded folks.

Departing me with a hug it was, "tell your daddy I love him and tell your mother she's beautiful". There was no end to it, the words being a continual hug. The power of his mind's tape player was a continual rocket launching—love and positive karma engulfing the moment, and he never changed. He came from humble means in Norfolk, Virginia, took President Carter on his fishing boat in his 40's, became a substitute Judge, an endless list and a big life lived. He was the late Attorney Pete Decker, my father's friend. How do you think your life will work out if you embrace a similar mindset? I'd say quite well. These souls seem to succeed at anything within their grasp. Revealing that what you tell yourself becomes your reality. Also, *Ask and you shall receive.* Evidence supports this. Yes the doors will open, but you must first TRY.

Have you noticed the confident posture and presence of the positive souls you admire most? Shoulders and head pulled back, a curious smile, eyes wide and ready for anything that comes their way—you'd think a nuclear missile couldn't take them down. They welcome challenges with open arms. Surround yourself with those who embody confidence and a can-do attitude, people whose service to others and their community is both sincere and radiates heartfelt intent. There is no *"I"* in *"team."* Make it a powerful, pervasive *"WE!"*

List Activities That Make You Feel Alive and Fulfilled

Based on my own experience, the following qualities will serve you well as you move forward: Confidence, Humor, and Humility.

Confidence: It is not something you are born with; it is developed over time, earned incrementally with each challenge you overcome after you TRY. Pushing yourself to the next level with intensity brings genuine fulfillment. When you align your purpose with passion—by fully sharing your gifts—you'll elevate your energy and reach your potential by again: TRYING. If you wake up excited about the day ahead, you're already on the right track.

Humor: Laughter is a medicine that has always pulled me through. Realizing that the past is gone and today is a new day can free you from unnecessary burdens. You operate at your highest levels when you are playful and open-minded. Avoid acting with a long face or taking yourself too seriously. Self-deprecation is one of the keys to success. If you are uptight, intense and serious you will break too easily. And, it is no fun.

Humility: True humility is the key to lasting success—it keeps ego and ambitions in check. It's not always the easiest people that teach us the most. Some of the most difficult individuals to work with—the ones who never apologize and are certain they know it all—show us a valuable lesson. Ultimately, those who think they know everything know very little. Ask yourself: will you spend your life playing a competitive game with others, constantly proving your worth, or will you create beautiful experiences—memories and meaningful connections that transcend mere competition? The choice is yours. The humble and quiet can remain a mystery and easy to be around.

Your attitude, perseverance, and refusal to quit or complain will carry you through tough times. Disappointments will always find you if you set expectations too high without thoughtful planning. Life is full of ups and downs; learning to adjust will keep you moving forward. Our catalyst is the saying, "insanity is doing the same thing and expecting different results."

Let's begin with some open-ended questions designed to encourage self-reflection. I encourage you to get a notebook that you can keep handy as you work your way through this book. Writing down your thoughts will help you get the most of out of the ideas expressed here.

Many of the following questions are subjective, and there's certainly a lot to consider, but this is your life. To uncover your mindset, identify the root causes of any discontent, or understand how things veered off course, self-discovery is absolutely essential. Our goal is to dig deep, getting to the very core of your feelings and soul, then uncovering the roots of your long-held belief system. From there, we'll discover what sparks your passions and fuels your specific motivational intent. What makes you feel ecstatic, elated, and energized to jump into action, operating at your A+ sweet spot? Is it something you've always loved, or something you've recently discovered? What obstacles are preventing you from making progress in this pursuit?

Conduct an honest intensive inventory of yourself and take on the necessary inner work. How do you come across to others—down-to-earth, even-keeled, haughty, arrogant, understanding, soothing? Let this be a luminous process for change. Your sincerity, positive attitude, and willingness to shift your outlook are crucial in this exercise, whether you move forward based on the suggestions here or in any other sources you're open to exploring.

We can go through a step-by-step process, but ultimately, it's up to you to focus and determine what's most important. From there, you'll define a scope of work and prioritize objectives to achieve your goals, placing your passions at the center of everything you do. As you make this plan, we'll address self-motivation and encourage self-reflection—both essential for setting and achieving personal goals.

If you follow through, all of this work will change the course of your life. You'll take an honest look at the good and not-so-good aspects of your current situation and create a plan for incremental progress. A transformation of significant change is certainly possible, and in many lives, change is the only option—and it's often a good one.

I encourage you to think and reflect on the feelings that arise as you plan a significant change. Some questions may provoke resistance, but by identifying and confronting that resistance, you'll make your greatest progress. Not enough people go through this process, because it requires brutal honesty and the confidence of a champion to inspire true change. However, in the end a much happier, more authentic version of yourself will evolve. The true you will slowly, incrementally, come to life.

There's no need to rush; rather, create a well-thought-out game plan that aligns with your beliefs and moral code, clearly delineating your scope and objectives. There's no need for excessive sharing with friends or colleagues, either—keep improvements to yourself and set progress markers as you clear each hurdle. The results will reflect your larger macro-vision. A colleague once said to me, "I spend 100% of my time working on the 20% of things I can control". Agreed, although the percentages could vary. He was the same who quipped, "There are some people who don't know what they don't know". And it makes you think about whether or not you love or dislike problem solving, or the need to control things.

In the end, life is all about how things make you feel deep within your soul—whether it's your productivity, environment, colleagues, travel, job stability, or comfort level with risk-taking. You are the only one who can honestly review this for moving forward. This exercise will help you assess the current quality of your life and your feelings about it. We must open our minds for true change. In retrospect, change is fun. And you may laugh at your old self, your limitations, lack of knowledge, curiosity and lack of energized effort.

Start by recalling the happiest days of your life. Think about the ordinary moments when you felt genuinely fulfilled or appreciated—not necessarily milestones like graduations, marriage, or the birth of a child.

Once you've identified these happy moments, open all channels and entertain the following important questions. Your answers will illuminate your status within the realm of self-awareness and self-assessment.

Reflect on Your Peak Moments
When were you happiest—fully alive and engaged? Were you creating, exploring, helping others, or immersed in a passion? Take a moment to write down those experiences. Were you walking the beach with family, making music, helping a friend who was going through hard times, woodworking, hiking, or working in a lab? Were you engaged in an exhilarating field or enrolled in school?

Identify What Drives You
Who surrounded you during those moments? What role made you feel in your element? Did you feel free yet in control? Are you a team player or a solo trailblazer? What specifically gave you the most euphoric feeling? Were you assertive in giving or taking orders, or were you content and laid-back?

Pursue New Possibilities
What's next on your list to try? Do you need funding or a test run? How much time and money are you willing to invest? Can you do a test run of your ideas in a low-cost fashion, perhaps via internet marketing or word-of-mouth?

Assess Your Mindset
Do you dive into projects headfirst or hesitate out of fear? What's your backup plan if things don't go as expected? How do you handle setbacks—anger, blame, or resilience? Do you need to preemptively warm up to tasks, or do you enjoy life on the fly? If a project fails, what are your backup plans—B, C, and D? How will you feel if B and C fail as well?

Embrace Change
Are you set in your ways or open to new challenges? Do you follow your own goals or seek external validation? The only competition that matters is with yourself. You don't have to stay confined to one lane; you can explore new, exciting possibilities. Nurture a thriving imagination grounded in reality.

Define Your Work Style
Do you prefer working alone or with a team? Can you multitask, or do you need help with marketing and outreach? If you lead, will you delegate or control every decision? Do you want to keep your business to yourself, or are you willing to share it with others and put yourself out there to a broader audience?

Evaluate Your Motivations
Is your goal financial success, personal fulfillment, or both? Will money bring deep joy, or will it never feel like enough? Is your life all about the experience and journey or do you focus on activities with high annual returns?

Commit to Growth
Are you comfortable with the status quo, or are you ready for change? Do you go all in, or do you hesitate? What steps will you take to reclaim your joy? Or are you motivated to make changes, even if you don't yet know how to begin? Do you ever say to yourself, "In everything I do, I go big," or do you feel the opposite?

Prepare for Reality
Can you handle financial or emotional setbacks? Will you keep business and personal life separate? What's the worst that could happen if you simply try? What changes in your current life are you willing to make to regain the happiness you felt in those joyful memories you've identified? Are you iconoclastic enough to challenge the long-held beliefs you cling to?

Overcome Fear
Does the unknown excite or paralyze you? Fear itself may be your greatest obstacle. If success means meeting inspiring people rather than financial gain, is that enough? Are you ready to create a specific plan to change your life? If so, are you motivated to follow through and achieve your goals without quitting, no matter what happens? When you pinpoint a mission's target, are you steadfast and laid-back, or extremely competitive on all fronts and acrimonious if results don't meet your exact expectations?

Own Your Ideas
Do you hold back out of fear or lack of confidence? Growth requires action—take the leap.

Years ago, I embraced a simple philosophy: *Design Your Own Life*. I often wonder how things might have unfolded had I stayed in a corporate job instead of forging my own path. The confidence I gained as an entrepreneur eventually led me to create a local cable TV show, which ran for several years. I highlighted outstanding students, showcasing their achievements in academics and athletics. I assembled a volunteer crew, filmed students in action, scripted interviews, and managed production. Years later, I saw some of those students making headlines—playing in the NFL or appearing on national late-night TV.

The show cost me nothing but my evenings and weekends. While I didn't receive monetary compensation, the experience of documenting their progress was incredibly rewarding. It also boosted their confidence and presence within the local community.

Running the show independently and making every decision myself greatly increased my confidence, too. Despite the absence of financial reward, the sense of accomplishment was immensely satisfying. It was the universe in motion—everyone wins in situations like this. Positive energy circulates, good karma builds, and the community is inspired. Perhaps those shows sparked others to go out and create something meaningful. I'll never know, but I'd like to think they did.

Following my experience with the TV show, and supported by my background in engineering and management, I started my own business in custom building. This career offered significant flexibility in scheduling but came with its fair share of expected stress. Up to that point, I had constantly questioned myself, refining the answers to the questions that led to this decision. Hundreds of times, I pondered, "What's the perfect job?" as I sought a work schedule that would allow for maximum flexibility and work-life balance. My priority was always to get things done with the least amount of stress.

That question helped me define an end goal and revealed an important truth: setting big goals takes the same amount of energy as setting small ones. Goals, whether big or small, are most comfortably achieved in manageable, bite-size increments. This is achieved by making small adjustments, persevering over time, and never sacrificing your core values or belief system.

As for me, I embraced a mix of interests that kept life interesting: engineering, building custom homes, songwriting, playing guitar, reading, singing, and traveling—these diverse passions kept me out of my comfort zone, never allowing boredom to settle in. And humor was always by my side. It's fortunate to be surrounded by people who can make you laugh—including yourself.

Ask yourself: what, deep in my soul will truly give meaning, purpose, and passion to my life? What specifically is the 'it'? What are the characteristics of the most authentic version of me?

Identify your deep passions—the ones that come as naturally as breathing, the things you dabble in now but wish you did more often. These could be endeavors you started years ago but gave up when other obligations interfered.

Once you've gone through your soul-searching—and remember to leave out money as a primary driving force—narrow down your list of passions to two or three. This process may take time, perhaps weeks or even months, but it's essential to do the work.

Narrow Down Your Choices and Embark on Your New Path

You've narrowed down your passions to two or three. Now, pick one to prioritize. This will be your mainstay: your steadfast focus, the career choice for now. The second and third choices can become hobbies or side hustles during your weekends or evenings. The money earned from them can go towards the start-up funding for your first choice.

With this small action, you have indeed begun. Any start, even the smallest baby step, is significant. This is your acknowledgment that a new course is underway. The adage "If you have a map, you can go anywhere" is undeniably true, yet most people will never take the time to even jot down the first step in their entire life. Without a map or plan, we tend to flounder. We end up stuck in a dreaded rut that seems endless. Many people trap themselves in careers or commitments they dislike, using them as a foundation to endlessly complain. Refusing to break free from this paradigm is like sinking into the suffocating depths of a bottomless quicksand. You must free yourself from self-imposed limits.

Yes, you can have it all. And the day you realize that only *you* have the power to make it happen is the day you experience true freedom. It's your Independence Day and Super Bowl victory wrapped into one. Ideally, that day is today.

This realization, along with your first small step forward, is worth a million bucks. That's how much your freedom and self-knowledge are worth. A deep, progressive feeling comes to life. As you fuel your mind with joy and positivity, notice how your reality begins to shift with optimism. A profound sense of change will take place, a tangible vibration settling into place. This is a powerful space to inhabit as you begin to rise, overcoming obstacles and setting yourself on the path to prosperity.

Part of designing your own life through incremental positive change is remembering which bridges to avoid, learning from past experiences where you've been burned. The goal is to become empowered as you gain a better understanding of your strengths and weaknesses. Perhaps you enjoy seeing this entire thought process and utopian lifestyle as a game: weaving a fabric, tailoring it as you go, connecting dots that work for you, and prioritizing what you're passionate about. You're testing ideas that have been gestating for months or even years. Believe it or not, all of this can be launched in one entrepreneurial endeavor, streamlined into the one thing you've always loved.

Your next step might be spending your evenings and weekends trying out ideas, spot-checking, and getting a feel for the terrain of a new and exciting quest. You have nothing to lose by trying—it's usually free. Send off questions via email, start conversations with others, share your ideas verbally or at a conference with like-minded souls.

Get the wheels moving as soon as you can. Write down your thoughts, send yourself an email with a to-do list, set and stick to completion dates. Or develop your own follow-up methods to keep things on track. Your determination will ultimately carry the day.

Your discipline and follow-through, linked together in a daisy chain of commitment, are crucial. Do what's practical, commit to it, and adjust as you go. If you need a team to reach your goals, start putting one together. As you discover new personalities in building a team, you might encounter unique challenges—people that don't fit together. But sometimes, opposites attract.

The goal is to create a smooth-running machine, with everyone contributing harmoniously. Lead carefully, not through subjugation, admonishment, or pontification, but by ensuring that everyone is treated as equals, listened to, empowered, and plays a vital role in the team's focus—never losing sight of the established goals. Create an environment where positivity flourishes, fueled by shared creativity. Be sure to praise those who consistently come through for you and champion their specific areas of expertise.

Dreams and imagination are free. It's okay to envision a bold future, nurture lofty aspirations, and encourage others to think BIG! Talking about dreams is one thing—taking action is what truly matters.

Our minds have a way of distorting or even erasing what we don't want to confront, disconnecting us from reality. Instead of facing challenges head-on, we often generalize, group things together, and quickly discard them—an easy escape that lets us avoid the discomfort of the moment. It may bring temporary relief, but in the end, nothing is truly addressed. Rationalize or confront.

Taking those first steps for me was: While working at the University of Virginia I narrowed down my evening hours to succinctly grow a new idea, try something entrepreneurially. At the copy machine one day a young Architect said, I know you have these ideas, so why aren't you doing it? I so loved her no nonsense quip. "Student Talents with Stephen Jacques" was born from a blank sheet of paper; the Cable TV show which supported local students and highlighted their achievements and ran for 3 years. Then in the evening working on architectural plans to hire a builder then sell the residence a few years later. And that process went on for many years as I became a custom builder. Don't worry stress reared its head at every turn. The 10,000 hour rule of devotion lives.

Embarking on your new path is huge once you've brainstormed and distilled your favorites. At age 25, to get out of my Virginia comfort zone, I drove cross-country to Hollywood and got into a few movies. Driving across the desert alone was quite an experience. Windows rolled down so AC wouldn't overheat. One film I participated in was with actor Joe Piscopo in "Dead Heat", filmed at a water treatment plant in Van Nuys, California. Years later, a part in the TV series "Homicide: Life on the Street" as a medic on a north Baltimore estate. James Earl Jones, the late great one, was at the lunch buffet with me. All of the cool things taking place when a casting agent rings or emails! But we must take those steps, with each iteration followed through. Detail after detail you have to get right in order for things to succeed.

Everything starts with a blank sheet of paper, your imagination, simply white space, air and sky in front of you. You create and imagine or....you guessed it, nothing happens.

2
BUILD PERSEVERANCE AND CONFIDENCE

The building blocks for confidence and perseverance are created over time, not something you can purchase, acquire or copy from others. Setting goals, following through, and holding yourself accountable lead to learned wisdom, a foundational base from which to launch your next move. Surrounding yourself with positive, like-minded souls lets you thrive.

THIS CHAPTER COVERS:

Developing a Winning Attitude
- *Embrace challenges and view them as opportunities for growth.*
- *Develop resilience by pushing through obstacles.*
- *Be careful what you think.*

Surrounding Yourself with the Right People
- *Seek out supportive and like-minded individuals.*

DEVELOPING A WINNING ATTITUDE

Embrace Challenges and View Them as Opportunities for Growth

Isn't it fascinating when you meet someone new—maybe an organic farmer, a photographer, or a music producer—and immediately sense that everything they touch will eventually succeed? It all turns to gold no matter what. It's strange how it resonates; you can just feel it in their presence. They exude confidence, always getting things done, seemingly on a mission known only to them. This confidence allows them to embrace challenges and view them as opportunities for growth.

You can't help but wonder: What drives them? What makes them tick? Their great achievements seem to come effortlessly, like a path they were always destined to walk. They come across as grounded and always seem to have their mind right. You feel inspired, even a little envious. At times, you might even catch yourself wishing you could be them.

How do these individuals manage to be so poised—so polished, charming, and smart? They have it all figured out. Who were their parents, or did they get here entirely on their own?

What you witness is a stable, grounded presence—a constant positive attitude that never wavers. It's as if they've discovered some secret potion, a recipe for success that only they know how to mix. Day after day, they seem to accomplish so much with nary a complaint. How do they do it? This shiny, astute embodiment of competence and clarity feels almost like a trained athlete, always in motion and achieving in real time.

And doesn't it seem like they go big with everything they do? Whether they're an expert chef, PhD student, or confidently navigating a field like landscape architecture, they excel at whatever they undertake. Like watching a bullet train hum along effortlessly at 200 mph. Where does all this drive and success come from, and how far will it go? You can't help but wonder—What will it take for me to do half of what they do?

Life isn't a competition, but these individuals are undeniably inspiring. Watching them in action is motivational. There's a magical energy, a positive buzz surrounding those can-do phenoms. I admire these types. If their energy were a drink, you'd want to have a gulp or two. But it's not just their energy—it's their attitude and outlook. Often, their parents were steady or solid as rocks, laying the foundation for this incredible force.

Watch their body language closely: it's not the timid or pessimistic slouch of someone filled with dread. No, their shoulders are pulled back, they maintain steady eye contact—purely focused. Inspiration seems to pour from them—teeming and alive. It's not an act. They're genuinely who they are, a product of years spent overcoming challenges, all while maintaining a positive outlook.

Unfortunately, confidence, a great attitude, or a complaint-free, productive soul can't be bottled or easily duplicated. There's always a path successful people have had to walk—a path you didn't see. And it wasn't always easy. It was earned. Yet, in the end, the takeaway is clear: You can become your own version of that inspiration. Each step, misstep, and adjustment will drive you forward. The best part is this: every new day is a fresh opportunity, but only if you bring your plan to it. Yesterday is gone. Today is here, waiting for you to make it yours.

Behind the scenes, the most capable people are often the hardest workers, and their path is built on the foundation of setbacks, challenges, and growth. Unfortunately, that road can also become filled with self-imposed roadblocks—sometimes knowingly, sometimes unknowingly—that hold back our own progress. It's almost as if we subconsciously prefer wallowing in difficulty, rather than stepping forward with confidence and action.

Remember, you are in charge—the Director of your thoughts. The more you feel in control, the more confidence you will cultivate. Your newfound confidence will resonate with others as you express yourself more fully and comfortably.

As you begin to set clear boundaries and stick to them, as you speak up with calm conviction, others will begin to see and respect your poised stance. They will feel your stability, confidence, and clarity, and this energy will inspire and positively affect those around you.

The energy you surround yourself with has a direct impact on your thoughts and decisions, ultimately influencing the outcome. Uplifting music, inspiring books, and laughter can shift neutral energy into positive flow within your body. By feeding yourself these elements, you set a unique vibration for your mind, body, and spirit. It's a full-circle cycle that elevates your energy, empowering you to face challenges with ease and find solutions that arise effortlessly.

When you truly know yourself and enforce the boundaries you've set, you achieve balance and focus. You are then ready to face whatever challenges come your way. Reflect on what intimidates or threatens you—what are the buried or underlying fears that stem from those feelings? Are they just irrational thoughts, cycling around like a broken record, or do they have roots in past experiences, especially from childhood, which are holding you back?

Think back to every major challenge you've taken on and consider the worst-case scenario. Reflect on all the decisions you made along the way. Ultimately, embracing challenges comes down to how you choose to respond. Traits like stubbornness, quick anger, or close-mindedness can halt progress if you let them. But openness, flexibility, and a willingness to listen create paths to growth and improvement.

DEVELOP RESILIENCE BY PUSHING THROUGH OBSTACLES

Entrepreneurs face failure all the time—they regularly test and try different approaches. It's not personal. It's just part of the process of learning, adjusting, and improving. You get better at decision-making by doing it repeatedly, and over time it becomes more natural, not dissimilar to playing a musical instrument. As you keep practicing, your processes and patience evolve. You begin to learn when it feels right to lean in, to take risks fearlessly, and to keep moving forward.

The key? Follow-through. Because quitting? Quitting only leads to starting over once again, without the lessons learned. Remember, persistence always pays off in the end, and setbacks are just an opportunity for you to course-correct and improve your approach. It's essential to remember your pitfalls because they were your lessons. It was never success that taught you, always failure.

Having grit, perseverance, confidence, and a steadfast focus is essential—keep it up. The truth is, things don't always go as planned. Sometimes, despite doing everything you could, the outcome isn't what you hoped for. In moments of setbacks, your reaction will be the defining factor. The real test lies in how you choose to respond. Take a deep breath, step back, and look at the bigger picture. Know that these moments are a natural part of life, and they happen to everyone. That alone can make a big difference in your mindset.

If a job, project, or endeavor doesn't work out, it doesn't mean you've failed. Don't make the mistake of labeling yourself a failure. Sometimes, the reality is that it's just not a good fit—with you, the organization, or the approach itself. And that's perfectly okay. Often, it's just about recognizing that some things don't align, and when that happens, it's a sign to move forward and try something new. In the face of loss or adversity, it's important to rebound with optimism.

In those challenging times, you often must be your own cheerleader. Pep yourself up with positive affirmations: "The best is yet to come." "Everything I touch turns to gold." "Wherever I go, I bring peace, love, and joy." When you repeat these thoughts each morning, it begins to influence the results of your day. The energy you give out into the world is a magnet for positive energy in return.

Don't get hung up on a single setback. Move past it quickly and efficiently—you're the only one dwelling on it. Beating yourself up over something that's already in the past is counterproductive. It's just one experience in a sea of many, and you can't change it. So, live in the present and stay hopeful. Keep your head up, have a bounce in your step, and embrace new opportunities with enthusiasm. A positive attitude and good health are invaluable—worth more than any monetary wealth.

And yet, there are events happening globally—wars, acts of terror, suffering—that can remind us how much larger the world is than our own trials. If you're experiencing difficulties in your life, know that you're not alone. Many are sending prayers for strength, healing, and hope.

Often what truly elevates a person is helping others. That's where the true genius lies. I experienced this sense of fulfillment when I fed the homeless during the holidays, cooking meals from cherished family recipes and distributing them from my car. It felt like a soulful connection with others. The gratitude shared by those individuals was deeply touching, and I found those moments more fulfilling than some family gatherings. It was a beautiful reminder that often, the joy you give others reflects back to you in ways you can't anticipate.

We're all in this together. The more we support one another and maintain perspective, the faster we can move forward—collectively and positively. When you face a setback, how you rebound is not determined by your immediate feelings. There's no rush—

take a deep breath and approach the situation strategically. Your response won't be filled with panic or uncertainty. Instead, you'll be prepared, armed with backup plans B, C, and sometimes D, all laid out in a reasonable, logical way.

To get started in switching to one of your backup plans, grab a pencil or use a scheduling app to map out your next steps. Avoid wasting time wallowing in self-pity or letting frustration take over. Remember: if you don't believe in yourself, others may not either. Don't depend on external validation—this is about doing it for you. By acting immediately, you'll take control and see progress. Trust that it will be done right when you follow through yourself.

When things feel overwhelming, retreat to quiet spaces. Use moments of solitude to regroup. Meditation and mindful moments feed your soul in ways far more nourishing than turning to substances. Life presents constant dichotomies, and your choice will define your path. Keep choosing wellness and resilience.

Be Careful What You Think

Being your own cheerleader in challenging times applies to both thought and action. If your inner dialogue is "Nobody in my family attended college, medical school, or acquired a significant piece of land, so it's surely impossible for me," this becomes the broken record in your mind—your replay tape. It becomes your constant companion and the foundation of your limitations. You start to embody those words, repeat those actions, and the cycle grows in strength. This self-talk stays ingrained in you, forming the "safe zone" that holds you back. But that narrative isn't set in stone; it's simply a habit—a tape you can choose to erase. Consistent action changes this tape.

Self-confidence is built through the experience of overcoming fear and stepping up to challenges, often with patience. Every hurdle becomes an opportunity for growth, and with each victory, your confidence grows stronger. Those who exude self-confidence become magnetic. People trust their grounded, steady presence and feel assured in their leadership. They're the ones with a clear mission, who are unshaken by fear and open to the possibility of what could be. They effortlessly walk away from situations that don't serve them, trusting that new opportunities will come. These confident individuals absorb potential, listen intently, and have an innate ability to formulate questions that open pathways to new ideas. Their minds are constantly turning, exploring the "end zone" of what's possible and how to make it a reality. They lead teams with knowledge, trustworthiness, and a steady hand into the unknown, with a plan firmly in place. Their positivity radiates through their eyes and their actions, fostering an environment where action and progress are the focal points.

Such individuals think in terms of what IS possible—not what isn't. They attract a network of like-minded individuals, moving beyond the noise of negativity. They actively pursue goals and have the ambition to see the world and make a meaningful impact. Their reputations are impeccable, built on honesty and integrity. These are the true achievers—the ones whose reputation precedes them and whose actions match their words.

Imagine waking up with Steven Spielberg's mindset, filled with confidence and ambition. He might start the day mentally plotting his next big project—creating several feature films over the next five years, working with talented actors and crews, and envisioning countless screenplays beyond that.

The same attitude can be applied to any dream or ambition. Someone might declare, "Next year, I'm buying that farm parcel, building my dream home, scaling my small business, and ramping up investments. It's all going to be fun and easy, and it's happening. I can't wait to make strides on all fronts with my family and friends."

So, what's stopping you from thinking and executing like Spielberg or other can-do visionaries? You are the director of your own story. The script you follow, the mindset you cultivate, and the path you take are entirely in your hands. If negativity creeps in, it's simply a cue that you've slipped into *bad director* mode, and it's time to rewrite the narrative and polish up the self-talk.

The real power lies in shifting your entire mindset. Many people dream of thinking like billionaires—not because of the money, but because of the mindset they believe it takes to achieve great success. However, some allow fear, bad habits, and irrational limits to overshadow their dreams. They might wake up feeling defeated or full of self-pity, allowing those emotions to control their day. Some even unintentionally will themselves into failure, wrapped in a cycle of complaints that offer a sense of false comfort. Do people like Spielberg associate with these kinds of mindsets? Likely not. If he ever encountered such negativity, he might offer some gentle support but walk away quickly, knowing that there's no time to waste on sinking ships. Spielberg understands that change begins with self-awareness—recognizing and altering your self-talk. This is the cornerstone of maturity and adulthood. Change your narrative and you change your reality. With clear, healthy thoughts and a positive mindset, your life transforms.

Nothing stopped Spielberg. What he had was persistence, creativity, and dedication—a clear vision with meticulous planning. Each decision he made, each tweak, each collaboration brought him closer to realizing his goals. The road was paved with hard work, and those who aligned with his drive and passion shared in that same triumph. Spielberg thrives in collaboration, adjusting his plans to bring out the best in the team around him. This honesty and adaptability fuel a vision that resonates with excellence.

Meanwhile, those stuck in negativity or inaction sit on the sidelines, unable to seize opportunities, whether it's for business, personal growth, travel, or education. Their complaints become their cage, keeping them confined while others move ahead.

The key difference lies in action—the ability to pivot, adjust, and move forward despite doubts or fears. Those who stay stagnant, resistant to change or unwilling to act, will miss out on nearly every meaningful opportunity. Everything worthwhile requires proactive engagement. You can't sit on the sidelines wishing for change; you must create it. It's all about imagination and vision. So, why not pursue your dreams, harnessing confidence and determination? Make it fun and happy.

Once you have a dream, the most important part is simple: *Start. Try. Try again. Reset.*

SURROUNDING YOURSELF WITH THE RIGHT PEOPLE

SEEK OUT SUPPORTIVE AND LIKE-MINDED INDIVIDUALS

Surrounding yourself with smart, sensible, and grounded individuals is key to success, no matter what area of life you're focusing on. Their sound advice, solid character, and genuine care are invaluable assets. If you choose your partners, business associates, colleagues, and friends wisely—looking for traits like character, integrity, humility, responsibility, punctuality, and resourcefulness—you'll have a strong foundation to build upon. And don't overlook *fallibility*. Recognizing that everyone has made mistakes but has learned from them is part of personal and collective growth.

We all love a winner, but life has a way of revealing your true friends when challenges arise. You'll likely be able to count them on one hand—no exaggeration. It might not even be their fault, but many will quietly disappear when times get tough. It's human nature to gravitate toward a winning team. That said, it's not the person with the most toys who wins in the end. If your only goal is to make money, that's probably all you'll have when all is said and done.

Perhaps the real value lies in the journey, not in accumulating material things. That's something you'll have to discover for yourself. Failure, believe it or not, is often the greatest teacher. It's as though you've attended a vibrant party where your vulnerabilities, missteps, and weaknesses are openly discussed. These "flaws" become your guides, helping you refine your approach and avoid pitfalls in the future.

Surround yourself with those who embrace learning and growing, as they know how to dance with failure gracefully and move forward with newfound wisdom. People who focus intently on the small details have their lives in order, and this kind of discipline contributes tremendously to success. Start each day organized and commit to tackling your hardest task first. Listen carefully, seeking wisdom and insights from those who know more than you, while also learning to invest in yourself. Through persistent effort and self-investment, you'll develop multiple talents and skills that will only expand with time.

When it comes to personal or business relationships, it's vital to streamline processes and eliminate "dead weight." Identify complainers, those who waste time, or those lacking integrity early on—and let them go. Parting ways may seem hard, but ultimately, it's beneficial to both sides. It saves you time and energy and ensures that your relationships and partnerships remain focused and productive.

Recognize that both rookies and veterans offer something valuable. Veterans bring wisdom and insight, honed over years, while rookies bring fresh energy and enthusiasm. Both are essential, depending on the task at hand. It's critical to trust your instincts. People who are shifty, dishonest, or ungrounded will reveal themselves quickly, usually through their behavior or body language. Trust your gut feelings. "Believe nothing you hear, and only half of what you see," a sentiment I often heard echoed by a wise coworker, holds up in many situations.

Keeping things simple is another key principle. Minimalism, in both business and life, allows you to focus on what truly matters. Assemble a tight-knit team of trustworthy, like-minded people with whom you share a strong rapport.

If you can't find someone to fulfill a particular task, take the lead yourself until you find a suitable replacement. You may find it challenging, but the hands-on experience will teach you lessons no textbook could. Every challenge you face and each step you take builds confidence and decision-making skills.

In moments of stress or setbacks, remain calm. Don't second-guess yourself. Growth is a series of gradual adjustments. Avoid spiraling into frustration, hopelessness, or other negative emotions. It's crucial to keep focusing on your desires and goals—on what **you** want out of this life. Overthinking can trap you in a cycle of inaction, wasting time and energy. Accept things as they come, adapt quickly, and move forward without hesitation. It's all part of the journey—stay patient with yourself.

Trust your gut, but don't get lazy. When you choose to "wing it"—neglecting details, offering sloppy analysis, or placing too much trust in someone—you're setting yourself up for problems. It's a scary prospect, to say the least. The more details you have or uncover in any situation, the better prepared you'll be. Ask probing questions to truly understand, and never underestimate the importance of digging deep. Life is full of uncertainties, and people can let you down, especially when your expectations exceed what they can give. This can be a tough lesson, but it's an important one. It's a reminder that if you're not making mistakes, you're not growing.

Focus on what truly matters to you and align your actions with how it makes you *feel*. If someone doesn't prove to be a good fit, don't waste time on the blame game—let them go. Ironically, we should almost thank others for the bad experiences they bring us. It's through these moments that you learn, grow, and ultimately avoid repeating the same mistakes. If you stay grounded in ethics, responsibility, and integrity, nothing will stand in your way. So, stay true to yourself. Keep your focus clear and your actions aligned with what matters most to you.

Looking back on my own journey, I cherished being surrounded by experts—those who were curious, humble, and got the job done. These people were hard to find, but when I did find them, their expertise and willingness to share made all the difference. Many of them didn't take themselves too seriously. That humility and playfulness is something everyone admires. To unlock possibilities, we must be willing to see ourselves as part of a larger story and remain open to the path ahead.

3
COMMIT TO HONESTY AND AUTHENTICITY

Authenticity and honesty are key to personal growth. Avoid self-sabotage by being truthful with yourself about your desires and goals. This commitment will anchor you as you navigate life's challenges.

THIS CHAPTER COVERS:

Committing to Honesty and Authenticity
- *Be honest with yourself—and others—about your current life and your goals.*

Maintaining Momentum
- *Set clear goals and take consistent steps toward achieving them.*
- *Stay focused and avoid distractions.*

COMMITTING TO HONESTY AND AUTHENTICITY

BE HONEST WITH YOURSELF—AND OTHERS— ABOUT YOUR CURRENT LIFE AND YOUR GOALS

When you approach any endeavor with full commitment to honesty and authenticity, the outcome is far more promising. Anything less than full dedication is a waste of your time and everyone else's. This commitment to authenticity, coupled with honest self-reflection and clearly defined goals, will serve as an anchor, creating the path to the life you desire.

Tapping into your authentic self, driven by instinct and enthusiasm, is where you begin to hit your stride. It's as natural as breathing, and there's no need to construct walls of fear or get caught up in the noise and opinions of others. Sure, people might not understand you the way you understand yourself, but don't allow them to dictate your life. Their advice, especially on serious matters, is often no more helpful than asking casual acquaintances for legal counsel. It's easy to slip into the comfort of negative self-talk and rely on external validation for your encouragement. But by continuing the cycle of seeking external validation from others, you'll never unlock the happiness or professional clarity you seek.

Fear-based anxieties and self-doubt often dominate the mind, especially early in life, but who is stopping you from changing your perspective? Nobody but yourself. The key to change is action—getting started is the hardest part, but every small step counts. The first step is a game-changer. A simple email to inquire about an idea, or a phone call to initiate a conversation, can build momentum that leads to real progress. These "baby steps" accumulate, and before you know it, the fear that once held you back is a thing of the past.

Often, we're told *NO* so many times that we seek refuge in helplessness, thus stalling any progress. But the crucial information you need to move forward is often freely accessible—whether through research or talking to experts. It's said that "ninety percent of genius is showing up to work." When you show up consistently, work hard, and embrace a laser-focused approach, mastery becomes inevitable. Dedicate yourself to the process, stay disciplined, and persist no matter what. The trouble with quitters and complainers is that they rarely make progress. They're perpetually starting over instead of building a solid foundation to operate from. Ownership of your path, coupled with dedication, is what leads to tangible results.

The first place to be honest is in examining your present situation. Does your job bring you joy, or are you simply going through the motions? Is there something more for you out there? Procrastination only holds you back from change—so don't wait! Life is too short to feel stuck. It's time to explore alternative opportunities: writing, coaching, teaching, or even pursuing a business idea that excites you. Writing these options down and analyzing the pros and cons can help uncover what's missing from your current life. Maybe it's a side hustle, a creative project in the evenings, or a social group that sparks inspiration.

Through soul-searching, you will begin to identify what brings you genuine happiness and what weighs you down. You may even find that making small adjustments to your current life—like joining a hobby group or reevaluating certain habits—could lead to major shifts. Connection is key. Realizing that you're not alone in your struggles is incredibly powerful.

Then, take stock of how your time is spent: commuting, family duties, your work—are you focused on what genuinely aligns with who you are or who you want to become? Don't procrastinate on making small adjustments to live a more balanced and authentic life. And if you find yourself stuck in a rut mentally or emotionally, it's essential to seek help. Just like seeing a doctor for a physical ailment, seeing a therapist for your mind is vital—your mental health fuels everything else. An enthusiastic life coach can help guide you, fine-tune your goals, and increase your motivation. If you can afford even one session, it will help.

As you evaluate your current life, stop holding yourself to outdated expectations from family or from old versions of yourself. Liberate yourself to move in new directions and take charge of your growth. You have the power to shape the course of your life at any moment—don't let old barriers limit you. It's time to thrive authentically, free from the weights of unnecessary rules or restrictions. Taking no action leads to stagnation—what some may call a "dead zone" where complacency sets in. If you find yourself there, it's important to recognize that even seemingly irreparable situations can improve with effort, persistence, and a fresh perspective. Perhaps in the past you've given up too quickly or felt discouraged after a few failed attempts. But these moments of perceived failure often arise from mislabeling the situation as something unchangeable, when in fact, change could be the very key to liberation.

The sooner we stop lying to ourselves, the sooner we start honing our craft and moving towards a well-defined direction. Pursuing things that aren't true to our essence is a waste of time, and recognizing those distractions is crucial for progress. Sometimes, a brief, casual conversation in a coffee shop or parking lot sparks a new possibility and shifts the trajectory of our lives. These seemingly small moments can ignite big changes and open our minds to broader horizons. Our limited imaginations and the failure to plan and act are often what hold us back.

As a young person, it's hard to know exactly what you want to be when you grow up; the options seem endless. At eighteen, you choose a college major with very little life experience to guide you. But life isn't about a set-in-stone trajectory—it's about adjusting along the way, doing what feels right, and learning how to deeply connect with what truly excites and fulfills you. True treasures come from deep self-reflection. When you take the time to go inward, taking stock of your heart and mind, you discover your own nirvana.

One of the most important truths to embrace is that without bold action, no progress can occur. The very idea of change can often be mistaken for stress, but change is an opportunity to improve—to let go of outdated modes of thinking and step into a more powerful version of yourself. It's through taking deliberate, courageous action that you make room for growth, possibility, and prosperity in your life.

Start by considering your options. Even the smallest of movements will start setting things into motion. Research your opportunities, target areas of interest, and explore possibilities. Network actively, both online and in your community. Utilize social media, join groups, or take courses that align with your passions. Treat the process of exploring as you would when making new friends—be curious, excited, and open to possibilities. You'll quickly realize that opportunities to improve, grow, and discover new passions are right before you, sometimes in unexpected places like your local community center, university website, or local bookstore.

Then, make your ideas tangible. Set a start date and actively pursue your ideas, one step at a time. As you start executing, you'll likely see a variety of doors open that you hadn't initially anticipated. The first step is simply to write down your thoughts, reflecting on your dreams, then turning them into a feasible strategy for success. By taking these small yet impactful actions, you've already begun your journey toward a more fulfilled life. Fresh inspiration and new opportunities will take shape as you actively move towards your goals.

Remember, change is never as daunting as it first seems—it's where transformation begins, leading you toward a richer, more satisfying experience of life.

MAINTAINING MOMENTUM

SET CLEAR GOALS AND TAKE CONSISTENT STEPS TOWARD ACHIEVING THEM

The process of executing—taking action—gradually becomes not only essential but enjoyable. Like a good cup of morning coffee, the effort becomes second nature, creating a consistent flow of new habits and empowering your journey. Investing in yourself through decisive actions helps mitigate future regrets and ensures you're progressing in meaningful ways. Each small step you take creates an amplified sense of accomplishment, one that elevates your vibration and spreads positivity, especially when you reflect on it with gratitude. When you realize that everything moving forward is directly tied to your own efforts and intentions—when you know your actions are backed by sincerity and kindness—you find a deep, nourishing sense of fulfillment.

Entering new territories or overcoming obstacles often requires us to be mindful of our tendency to place self-inflicted speed bumps in our paths. Procrastination, self-sabotage, or creating hurdles where none need to exist comes from insecurities or an internal need to avoid discomfort. This mindset of delaying action, making excuses, or wallowing in regrets keeps us stuck in a perpetual loop.

It's crucial to recognize that some people, especially those who prefer a laid-back lifestyle, don't measure success in typical milestones, and they can also inspire us. Their route may be circuitous, creative, or reflective of a slower decision-making process, perhaps coming from insecurities or an inclination to control their environment. In some cases, such people excel in unconventional ways despite not embracing deadlines or traditional timelines. Similarly, analytical types—detail-oriented and overly cautious—can tend to spiral into endless analysis. However, neither of these approaches should be a reason to dismiss progress. All personalities and methods offer value when understood.

The main takeaway is to remain grounded in your goals. Understand that speed bumps often signal a lack of confidence in your path, possibly linked to doubts or uncertainties. Taking a step back to assess why you're hesitating can open new doors to clarity. Question: Why am I doing this? If it's not driving progress, what's really holding you back? Deliberation, research, and planning are vital parts of the journey, but they mustn't hinder your forward motion.

The key is eliminating self-imposed barriers and focusing on action fueled by conviction. Ultimately, your attitude and motivation will guide everything you do. When you are driven by purpose and a clear focus, every challenge becomes a stepping-stone, every delay becomes an opportunity for reassessment, and every step forward is a reason to be grateful. Shift your mindset from contemplating what could go wrong to anticipating and creating what can go right. That's the key to unlocking fulfillment and sustained success.

If you can dream it and visualize it, you're already on the path to making it happen. But you need a road map. "Ask and you shall receive" is not just a mantra; it's a truth often realized in life. But remember, it's you, and only you, who must open the door. If you don't TRY, if you don't take risks, then nothing will change. Focus your mind, visualize your goals, and align your energy. With clear thoughts and positive intentions—manifesting good karma and clear skies—you will find that delightful surprises emerge in your life. Ask yourself: are you dreaming big enough, or are you setting cautious expectations that avoid risk to spare yourself disappointment?

When you create clarity around your goals and take consistent steps to achieve them, your life will transform. Warren Buffet once said his clarity to move forward from a poor stock or life decision came from "emptying the bathtub". It's gone, down the drain, learn from it—move on. It's nothing personal, just one of thousands of decisions, and if you get the big decisions right, it will pay off well in the long run. That billionaire probably knows what he's talking about.

STAY FOCUSED AND AVOID DISTRACTIONS

Life is filled with challenges that test both our emotions and our resilience, especially when you're trying to achieve personal and professional goals. Whether you're advancing in business or navigating personal matters, setbacks and hurdles are inevitable, often threatening to disrupt momentum when things seem to be on track. These hurdles can sometimes deflate your spirit, but they are simply part of the process. The key is to address them head-on, avoiding the traps of procrastinating or dwelling on frustration and refocusing on your end goal.

When I find myself stuck, my best antidote is simple: just do something. In the long term, let's look at doing something dynamic and huge, always thinking big, yet limiting risk. In the meantime, take a small, positive action: a workout, a phone call to a friend, starting a new hobby, researching a business idea, reading that book gathering dust. Every forward motion, no matter how small, fuels progress. Don't be afraid to venture into something new—it could be a valuable learning experience that leads to unexpected growth and success. By keeping your eyes and heart open to emerging opportunities and following through decisively, you will eventually reach your goals. The road isn't always smooth, but persistence and purposeful action make it possible.

Building and maintaining momentum is essential. Every time we overcome a challenge, it becomes an opportunity to strengthen ourselves further and refine our approach. Setbacks are simply speed bumps. By maintaining a clear, focused mindset and strategically planning, you can power through them smoothly, avoiding unnecessary delays.

A well-organized plan sets the framework for productivity. Setting goals and tasks with definitive timelines allows your efforts to align purposefully. Commitment and concentration are paramount, and when your actions are driven by a deep belief in your path, that energy amplifies your progress. Your mindset should reflect the determination to manifest your desires—focusing on achieving your goals, whether personal or professional, with laser precision.

Procrastination can be a major enemy on this path. Sticking to what's comfortable and avoiding the next necessary step in life is a form of self-sabotage. Often, the biggest hurdle is the subconscious fear of failure or an ingrained habit of avoidance. While we can learn from failure, staying stagnant in a comfort zone only breeds more hesitation and frustration.

To break out, it's essential to change your routine and shake things up. Exercising, learning new ideas, engaging with people, taking time for reflection—each of these practices can redirect your focus and energize your spirit. Pursue fitness goals that energize you both physically and mentally, and soon you'll notice the positive momentum spilling over into other aspects of life. Others who notice your amazing listening skills, compassion and character may hire you based on your outstanding values, presence, poise, and integrity. With those prized and ethical elements, you're unstoppable!

Collaboration with like-minded souls is both energizing and enjoyable—sharing your perspective and inner lens will inspire and uplift. To refuel and reset, cultivate a home environment that brings out the best in you, and nurtures a positive mindset and feeling. Surround yourself with music, incense, plants, flowers, laughter, or the joy of cooking or playing an instrument. Above all, embody and share the profound power of love in everything you do and say. Words carry immense power—use them wisely.

Maintain focus by structuring your days with a purposeful schedule. Keep both short-term and long-term goals in sight, as each small step forward contributes to meaningful progress, fueling motivation and strengthening your drive toward your ultimate vision. There is no right or wrong, address what is surfacing as a priority, go with your gut instincts.

4
OVERCOME PROCRASTINATION AND MENTAL BARRIERS

Procrastination and mental barriers often hinder progress. Address these by setting clear goals and maintaining a positive mindset. Embrace change and challenge yourself to grow continuously. Understanding your own personality will help you develop strategies for making progress toward your goals.

THIS CHAPTER COVERS:

Overcoming Procrastination
• *Identify reasons for procrastination and tackle them head-on.*
• *Break tasks into manageable steps.*

Digging Deep into the Unknown
• *Explore new ideas and opportunities without fear.*

Analyzing Personality Types
• *Understand your personality and how it affects your behavior.*
• *Adopt strategies to work with your natural tendencies.*

OVERCOMING PROCRASTINATION

IDENTIFY REASONS FOR PROCRASTINATION AND TACKLE THEM HEAD-ON

If you've been caught in a cycle of being over-enabled or spoiled—whether by parents or others—it's crucial to recognize that those days are behind you. It's time for a reset. Let go of the past—the times when you were overly cared for, shielded from hardship, or encouraged to take the easy road. Instead of seeing those experiences as limitations, view them as lessons. Perhaps your caregivers wanted to spare you struggles because they faced their own growing up. Acknowledge the love and kindness behind their actions. But now, the present moment is yours to shape. Your path forward is in your hands.

It's crucial to move forward, acknowledging that the past is only as relevant as the lessons it teaches, not as a crutch or excuse. The key is discipline—taking responsibility for your own actions, implementing new habits, and starting from wherever you are to build something meaningful. You have everything to gain by adopting the mindset that your achievements and outcomes are entirely based on your own efforts. The dreams you're working toward are solely fueled by your actions, perseverance, and focus.

It's also important to develop the strength of character that allows you to laugh at past mistakes, even seeing them as stepping-stones that have brought you precisely to where you are today. You weren't aware then, but you know better now. Don't linger on what could have been or blame others for challenges—everyone has their own struggles. Focus on where you are now and what's in your control. When you reflect on your mistakes, do so from a place of understanding and growth—not self-pity. To be habitually stuck in a loop of never finishing is a daily choice.

I once heard a famous motivational author respond to a long-winded excuse with a simple, "Is that right?"—then silence. That pause spoke volumes. We can justify anything if we believe our own BS, clinging to a one-sided, narrow perspective as if we hold all the answers. It's human nature to rationalize mistakes, building a mental case to shield the ego. But real growth comes when we challenge our own narratives instead of defending them. Thoughts are only thoughts.

Remember that there are no absolutes and no points for perfection. If your procrastination or lack of drive seems rooted in being too well taken care of in the past, it's important to recognize that. However, the moment to act is here, now. Don't be swept into thinking that the past is an excuse to procrastinate on opportunities or challenges in the present. We have only the present moment—how we choose to act today shapes the future. By admitting to ourselves that it's not the lack of time, but our choice not to act, we take power over our lives.

If you are neurodiverse or have had a diagnosis of ADHD or similar condition that features procrastination as a coping mechanism, adjust yourself to this information and persevere. Research and test out strategies to compensate for your way of working. There's a wealth of information out there, and many of the world's most accomplished people have achieved success by learning how to effectively work with who they are. See "personality types" below for more on how to work with your natural tendencies and ways of processing information.

Recognize self-imposed barriers. The mind has a way of rationalizing inertia, telling us there are reasons to delay. It could sound like "I don't have the time" or "I'm not ready yet" or "This isn't the right time for me." The truth might be that we've not yet decided to go all-in or be assertive enough to make something happen. Commitment, effort, and action take time, but they create the momentum needed to change everything.

Make no more excuses about not having time to pursue dreams, not being ready, or putting things off until "later." Start with one small step forward—this one choice can lead to amazing momentum. When you change how you spend your days, you change your future. Learning to get out of your own way is a game-changer.

How do these reflections align with where you are in your journey right now? Are you seeing areas where you could take more ownership of your progress? Improvements feel great when enacted.

Break Tasks into Manageable Steps

Baby steps can prove to be giant steps in disguise. By breaking tasks into smaller, more manageable parts and committing to steady, incremental progress, you can achieve meaningful and sustainable outcomes. Moving slowly through a well-thought-out approach can indeed move mountains. It's better to proceed slowly with steady progress than to unknowingly place roadblocks that hinder your forward momentum. So, consider taking very small steps forward, especially with tasks or goals you've been procrastinating on.

Start by committing to just one small item of progress each week. Write down a checklist of ten things, and cross them off as you go. Positive energy and the release of endorphins often accompany this process. Endorphins are defined as "hormones produced in the brain that act as neurotransmitters to relieve pain, improve mood, and increase feelings of well-being." The importance of a deliberate and thoughtful approach to progress cannot be overstated. Start with small tasks, executing them one by one. Don't fear thinking big and imagining huge possibilities. You'll get there, if you'll just start doing it!

It has been said that the hardest thing to do is to think, better yet, to think clearly. Our thoughts each day can inefficiently digress from one thing to another in random loops. Combat this tendency by defining specific targets, even those that may feel like a stretch. Dreaming big is not a violation—grant yourself a free life pass to dream bigger than big, then next month ramp it up again to an even bigger vision. Once the mental muscle that controls dreams and big ideas begins to take shape and blossom, your imagination will come alive magically, teeming with new ideas and nurturing fortuitous results.

Think back—didn't everything or everyone you admire who succeeded usually start small and humble? Typically, either a highly motivated, detail-oriented, or critical thinker was behind the formula. How did giants like Amazon and Nvidia skyrocket and explode? Look at their vast retail or technical competition. Consider the forces in marketing—diametrically opposed forces in an ever-changing open market of capitalism. Think about the mindset and macro-perspective of CEOs navigating economic vicissitudes while setting price points.

Do you think they tried fifty different concepts or out-of-the-box ideas while developing their products and processes? Do you think they were can't-do complainers or get-it-done scrappy tech folks with more grit than could ever be measured? Yes, there was a team, but who were the architects of that team? How many failures and disagreements were hammered out and incorporated along the way? How many competitors threw roadblocks into their paths, impeding progress, lying to them, misleading them, or attempting to steal their ideas, only to eventually disappear? Those who achieve big dreams have encountered those big roadblocks and more.

Irrepressible serial entrepreneurs ignite the spirit of capitalism and somehow figure it out. It's no different than a quarterback winning multiple Super Bowls—winners figure out a way to win when the stakes are high and everything is on the line. "Big-time players make big-time plays in big-time games," as the late football coach-turned-commentator John Madden often quipped.

John was one of a kind, had a vision, vast experience from the sidelines, and a big-picture view of the game and world. He picked up on the small details, communicating all of this with his warm genius humor to millions of viewers. Madden was bigger than life, and as my dad used to say, "He's better than the game." He carried gratitude along the way and was completely true to himself—there wasn't a phony bone in his body, despite his comical, self-deprecating nature. TV holiday games run replays of him as they'll never find another John.

We can all learn from this. Don't fake conversations. Be yourself. The world will love you for the one-and-only, authentic you. We are all much better off with more genuine, real-deal John Maddens, Oprah Winfreys, and Meryl Streeps. They blazed a trail, put in more than 10,000 hours, and remained true to themselves, their purpose, and their dedication to their craft. For me, just saying their names brings a powerful uplifting jolt of energy to the moment.

DIGGING DEEP INTO THE UNKNOWN

Explore New Ideas and Opportunities Without Fear

Embrace insightfulness, for it is the essence of true profundity. We must remain steadfast in our quest to uncover the deeper truths of existence. Rising above the limitations we impose upon ourselves, allowing the brilliance of new perspectives to illuminate our path. Your ideas!

As we challenge antiquated paradigms, forge ahead on a trail of your own making, mindful of the joy that accompanies your journey. Habitual self-restraint is a cycle that demands disruption. Liberation entails bidding farewell to anxieties rooted in fear and stepping boldly into the realm of possibility. It is about liberating our minds from the shackles of external validation, marching forth with unwavering resolve, and being unfettered by the constraints of societal expectations.

It is futile to dwell on matters beyond our control. Instead, we must embrace the freedom of fresh beginnings. Our true essence transcends external judgment. Free yourself of the past— it's gone.

Your imagination is infinite. It is the driving force behind all desires, ideas, and planning processes. Set aside opinions, judgments, and politics. Take time to reflect on the accomplishments of incredible minds like playwright William Shakespeare, actors Bette Davis and Katharine Hepburn, and Supreme Court Justices Sandra Day O'Connor and Ruth Bader Ginsburg. Consider figures like Thomas Edison, Steve Jobs, Jeff Bezos, and the prolific mind of James Joyce, whose prose seems superhuman to the average comprehension. Each of them showed us the way, leaving monumental footprints.

Regardless of how others are critiqued, we have no idea of the innumerable challenges they overcame. Where did their immense talent and confidence come from? Seemingly, it was a decision to unleash their deepest feelings and thoughts, allowing creativity to flow freely like an uncaged animal's true expression.

I remember writing some songs a few years ago and thinking, "There's more than one Bob Dylan out there. They just haven't released themselves to execute." It's okay to experience that yourself. Obviously, this isn't a competition, but it's our stunted imagination, weak limitations, and fear of disappointing ourselves that have us setting the bar too low—for both short-term and long-term goals. The child within us doesn't want to disappoint the child who believes in us. It's about protecting our hearts, egos, and the person we've labeled ourselves to be.

After we try something new, isn't it funny how, for the most part, nothing dreadful happens? The negativity and its nonsense were simply exaggerated drama in our minds—on guard, protecting us from something that never materialized. Remember: no fear!

Considering what your parents did for a living and where they focused their efforts, you might think, "I've seen this movie already." Surely their paths had ups and downs like the rest of us. However, your imagination will be the key to everything. If you ever feel empty of ideas, look to your most successful family members, friends, or business associates—those who seem to be on fire, achieving in every way known to humankind. Are they calling you or are you calling them, and why is this so?

Note here: You will be them ... eventually, when you decide to: Do the things that must be done to become the new you. You aren't going to copy their playbook, but you can certainly take notes on their actions and approaches and test out similar moves. Once you're well-positioned and feeling grounded with traction, things will take off like a rocket, provided you maintain a positive attitude and refuse to quit. If you give up on this, you'll likely give up on the next challenge. Stay committed to the entire journey, even when things seem unbearable.

This holds true if you are committed and aligned with things you genuinely love and find meaningful. If you have a passion for something, you'll likely excel. But if you can't stand it or your heart isn't in it, the outcome will likely be unfavorable.

Find your specific niche and that well-thought-out sweet spot, then work it diligently. Keep exploring options. Step outside your comfort zone to where exciting new opportunities await. Creating something from a blank sheet of paper through self-motivation and creativity pays off, often in ways you would never expect. Ultimately, your manifested ideas, combined with a strategic approach, will produce a sense of fulfillment upon completion.

Once you have landed on a new opportunity to explore, you must commit to consistently following through. Don't drop the ball. Bring each element to fruition by demonstrating attention to detail. Allow yourself to dream big, taking calculated risks one at a time and setting precise timelines and benchmarks. Plan vacations or short breaks to decompress and avoid burnout. This is not a race; this is your well-planned journey, lived to its fullest.

ANALYZING PERSONALITY TYPES

UNDERSTAND YOUR PERSONALITY AND HOW IT AFFECTS YOUR BEHAVIOR

Understanding ourselves better paves the way for healthier relationships. It helps us become more cooperative, positive, and enjoyable to be around. Self-reflection and self-awareness shape how others perceive and interact with us.

Now consider this: what happens if we're unpredictable or prone to explosive reactions, holding on to disappointments until we unleash them verbally? Do you know someone like that? How would you feel if the roles were reversed? Can you genuinely see things from others' perspectives, or are you fixated on your own? Sometimes, it's necessary to step back, reassess, and readjust.

Here are a few questions to reflect on:

- Are you a self-starter, or do you rely on others to push you forward? Are you improving?

- Can you carry your own weight, or do you often need support? What's holding you back?

- If you were brutally honest, how would your closest friends describe you? Laid-back, positive, passive-aggressive, aloof, nosy, joyful, rude, pedantic, confrontational, neglectful, loving, peaceful, narcissistic, or genuine?

- What drives you more—money or the journey? A mansion or a beach in France?

- If you received your dream home today, would you still feel unfulfilled?

- Do you sabotage a peaceful walk in the park or along the beach by dwelling on the past?

In the broader pursuit of happiness, consider how celebrity culture or media defines success, greatness, or joy. These societal projections often influence us more than we realize. Remaining true to yourself is vital, focusing on your unique path and goals rather than letting others dictate your choices. After all, what others say or do to you does not define you—it's your response that ultimately shapes your character.

Adopt Strategies to Work with Your Natural Tendencies

Reflect on your childhood and recall the activities that came naturally to you. Perhaps it was painting in art class, playing piano concertos, or excelling in a sport you loved but eventually drifted away from. Take a moment to consider these possibilities and reconnect with the ones that gave you the most meaning.

A friend once said, "mediocrity sucks." While I wholeheartedly agree, everyone has their own perspective. For me, anything I pursued with intensity and took to the next level added immense value and meaning to my life—whether it was touring a new country, watching foreign films, visiting museums abroad, enrolling in educational courses, or engaging in challenging sports. These experiences enriched my understanding, broadened my worldview, and unleashed a limitless imagination filled with possibilities.

Cross-cultural exposure, learning a new language, or traversing a new ocean doesn't just add to your skill set—it fosters personal growth. Go out and see the world! We are not promised tomorrow. The choice is simple: either get busy living or resign yourself to stagnation. In the process, you can choose to become wounded by setbacks or grow wiser because of them.

Never confine yourself to a singular identity. Avoid labeling yourself, others, or situations—these perceptions are shaped by your own mindset. Just as it would be a mistake for an artist at heart to suppress their creativity after studying the sciences, it's equally limiting to define yourself by a single title or role. Instead, explore the possibilities that genuinely spark your curiosity. Think back to the last five excursions you took, books you read, or events you attended. How many felt like a complete waste of time? How many would you truly take back? Likely, very few—if any. Every experience, big or small, contributes to your personal growth.

Engage with people who share your passions—you'll find common ground to share ideas, challenge one another, and critique projects. Networking, suggesting professionals, or simply exchanging perspectives can uncover opportunities you never knew existed. Start by finding your niche—the area where you feel confident, curious, and inspired. Immerse yourself in learning and discerning what fits you best. Entrepreneurs, for example, don't see trial and error as failures or setbacks. They focus on the insights gained and remain undeterred by unmet expectations. Life is not a competition where one must lose for another to win. Taking that mindset is a slippery slope.

Set a goal to meet someone new every week. Expand your circle, and approach interactions with an open mind. Opportunities often arise when you least expect them, but they require you to be curious, present, and proactive. When something feels right, act on it. The momentum you build will lead to growth, self-discovery, and a life lived with purpose. Make notes on progress: Journal!

5
TAKE RESPONSIBILITY

Learning from your experiences without placing blame is crucial. Focus on personal growth by maintaining a positive attitude and taking responsibility for your actions.

THIS CHAPTER COVERS:

Avoiding Self-Pity
- *Refrain from dwelling on negative experiences.*
- *Focus on solutions rather than problems.*

Breaking Mental Barriers
- *Challenge limiting beliefs and replace them with empowering ones.*
- *Push beyond your comfort zone.*

Challenging Yourself
- *Set ambitious goals and work diligently to achieve them.*
- *Continually seek self-improvement.*

AVOIDING SELF-PITY

Refrain From Dwelling on Negative Experiences

One of the greatest gifts you can give yourself is the ability to avoid self-pity when faced with disappointments. Instead, direct your focus inward. Why is it so common to blame or criticize others rather than reflecting on our own actions? Life offers countless lessons in attitude, patience, and perspective. Consider how often we tell ourselves that something is impossible. Is it because family or friends haven't succeeded in similar endeavors? Or perhaps we've grown comfortable with negativity, becoming what some might call "happy moaners."

Over time, walls of fear and doubt can build within the subconscious. These barriers can become traps, creating a false sense of helplessness. It's easy to settle into this space—a slow dance with negative self-talk that pulls you further from achievements and exciting new goals. Reiterating that, "It's easier to stay in a rut than to get out of one."

When confronted with a challenging question that feels overwhelming, do you see it as a personal attack or as an opportunity to think differently? Do you ever think that *the world is out to get you*? What if challenges are meant to encourage you to think bigger, step outside your comfort zone, and break down mental barriers? What if they're subtle prompts to explore new possibilities, dream beyond your perceived limitations, revealing the endless array of options available to you?

We sometimes avoid setting big goals to shield ourselves from disappointment. It's no wonder New Year's resolutions often become the subject of jokes—aspirations discarded almost as quickly as they're made. Thoughts like, "Dad and Mom never did that" may creep in and convince you to stay within the status quo. But don't become your own worst enemy. Always challenge yourself. Changing your mindset takes time, but it's worth the effort. Remember, the biggest obstacle standing in your way is often you. Shift your mindset and you will change the direction of your life!

Focus on Solutions Rather Than Problems

Are you truly happy? Or, upon honest reflection, are you afraid of allowing yourself to experience true happiness? Have you unintentionally created roadblocks that prevent you from fully embracing joy? Perhaps someone close to you negatively influenced your mindset, instilling sadness or pessimism.

But remember, you are not defined by the words or behavior of others—their actions are merely something for you to observe. It's crucial to block out the weight of a dark past, negative memories, and unchangeable associations. Instead, focus on cultivating an inner drive and creating experiences that promote genuine happiness. Focus on solutions rather than problems.

If thinking is the most challenging thing we do, let it be about exploring, discovering new areas of interest, and diving into the vast, exciting unknown. Prioritize endeavors that inspire forward motion and leave behind what doesn't serve you. Dwelling on financial struggles or perceived limitations only reinforces obstacles and prevents progress. Many find themselves stuck in a loop, telling stories about why things can't be done—feeding a self-perpetuating cycle of defeatism. Negative self-talk erodes confidence and, over time, can sabotage a meaningful life. Break free from this pattern. Redirect your thoughts toward positive outcomes and possibilities. Stop memorializing past hardships and focus on creating a future filled with victories and achievements. It's all about adopting a mindset of winning.

Why do successful or competitive athletes exude energy and hopefulness? Because they tackle every challenge with resilience, having built a habit of winning—it's simply their way of life. This same mindset can be applied to anything you pursue. But too often, disappointments and failures create a cycle of negative thoughts, embedding a fear-based memory loop—like a tape recorder replaying past mistakes. Instead of letting these thoughts control you, confront them. Set aside time to sit with your fears, recognize them for what they are—just fleeting thoughts—and then let them go. Release anything that no longer serves you and move forward with clarity and confidence.

Nothing in daily life is unchangeable. Perspective is malleable, and this is your power. Fear-based thinking, like a persistent organism, can take root, but it's your job to block out that noise. Remain focused, grounded, and resolute, especially when life's inevitable storms arise. Resist the temptation to dwell on past failures or negativity and use focus as your foundation for growth and progress.

When planning to do what you truly love, dedicate adequate time and effort to creating a thoughtful, actionable game plan. View it not as a burden but as an exciting challenge—a game you're ready to win. My father used to say, "Get in the middle of the problem." Ignoring issues won't make them disappear. Instead, address them directly, break them down into manageable details, and tackle each one head-on. Progress begins with action. Getting things moving each morning sparks a cascade of forward momentum, propelling you toward accomplishments. Remember, investing in yourself is the greatest thing you can do. It is what defines you. In this case, discipline and perseverance are 'in play'.

BREAKING MENTAL BARRIERS

CHALLENGE LIMITING BELIEFS AND REPLACE THEM WITH EMPOWERING ONES

Some people default to sadness and complaints, ingraining these bad habits in their minds over time. Whether knowingly or unknowingly, they box themselves into a corner where positivity, happiness, and joy become seemingly foreign concepts. The famed hilarious "Debbie Downer" skit on Saturday Night Live fits them to a "T"; Often, and sadly, where truth is stranger than fiction.

It's a thought-provoking question: do people truly change? Most habits are indeed formed at a young age, and some traits may even appear to be genetically predisposed. Reflect on old friends and their youthful achievements—their ambition, attitudes, poise, part-time jobs, and even body language. You might notice a strong correlation between those traits and their life habits today. With good reason: habits developed in youth often predict future outcomes.

But your destiny is not written in stone. Discipline, attention to detail, and ability to execute a plan while finishing what you start, can pay off in significant ways. Equally important is knowing when to say "No" —walking away when necessary.

Reprogramming your self-talk is crucial. How do you start your day? Do you instinctively grab your phone, scroll, or begin with organizing your room, meditation, brisk walk, a healthy meal? Do you take twenty seconds to smile in gratitude upon waking? Setting clear intentions and follow through with what you plan to achieve each day? Are you consistently pushing yourself to new heights, or do you hesitate because of fear, lack of confidence, or patterns of procrastination? These are questions to approach with brutal honesty. Understanding the driving forces behind your behaviors and mindset—be it fear, a lack of confidence, or ingrained habits of avoidance—can help you transform ephemeral patterns into lasting, meaningful growth. Reading books and discussing motivation is a great start, but YOUR specific action and effort awaits! What are you doing today, not tomorrow, to get the ball rolling?

Let go of what holds you back. Turn the page to the next chapter of your playbook. Life's complexities often demand custom solutions. If tailored by you and for you, these solutions should bring true happiness and absolute fulfillment. You deserve happiness, so stop denying it to yourself. Remove the obstacles draining your energy. You are the only one who knows each!

If a family member is acting as a mental roadblock hindering your growth, learn to bypass them without guilt. Ignore nonsensical barriers curtailing your progress and start living your defined purpose. Decide what's best for you and let others make their own choices. Be grounded in who you truly are, unshaken and undictated by the expectations or opinions of others.

On the flip side of this coin, avoid meddling in the lives of others. While helping someone may seem noble, it can backfire if you cross boundaries; they may even end up blaming you for interfering. Micromanaging others is a time-waster that seldom ends well. Instead, focus on your own path. Clear your mind to adopt a logical, goal-oriented mindset. Focus on what truly makes you happy and aligns with your personal goals. Discover your voice, whether through writing, teaching, public speaking, singing in your car before performing on stage, or becoming a leader in your community. Maybe you'll start a club of your own creation. The key is taking the first step—the simple act of trying—and then pressing the GO button.

Focus on what brings out the best in you. Reflect on what your specific goals can achieve and whether that outcome will satisfy you. Happiness awaits at the end of your journey, but you must own it all: the good, bad, and everything in between. Be willing to put in the effort and take advice from the best in each field. Your work, perseverance, and willingness to step forward will carve the path toward living a fulfilling and joyful life. Grab a pen, brainstorm some ideas on a note pad.

Push Beyond Your Comfort Zone

Familiarity and comfort zones, while appealing, can eventually feel confining. Predictable routines can offer security, but they may also inhibit growth. Simplifying life has its place, especially as we age, but it's the pursuit of new experiences and challenges that enriches life. Take calculated risks, push past self-imposed limits, and explore uncharted territory to feed your spirit and expand your world. Whether you travel to unexpected destinations, develop a new skill, or set bold goals, these actions fan the flames of passion and purpose. Complacency or action?

Just remember to maintain balance. As you chase success, prioritize self-care and nurture relationships. Positive energy shared with others often finds its way back to you, amplifying your joy and creating a cycle of mutual upliftment. Karma positivity *always* rotates, cycles back to you!

Needs and goals rooted deeply in meaning and purpose bring an authentic sense of fulfillment as you achieve them. Stepping beyond your comfort zone to realize your potential often leads to remarkable revelations. These moments may involve touching the lives of others through contributions and hard work or discovering *your people*—a community of like-minded, inspiring souls who encourage and elevate your journey. Their cumulative ideas shared are endless.

Fill your weekly schedule with meaningful activities, surrounding yourself with positive, supportive individuals. Explore new opportunities and embrace challenges, becoming a sponge for knowledge and change. Seek out what excites you—what gives you a sense of exhilaration. Even if you find it's not a perfect fit, you will not regret having tried. Like the clarity and elation that follow a great workout, these experiences renew your mind and spirit. Interesting folks abound.

Learn to find comfort in solitude—to simply BE. Much like meditation, this quiet practice builds inner strength, helping you remain present while shedding the weight of the past. Immerse yourself in serenity: a room lit by candlelight, the peaceful embrace of a garden, or the tranquil path of a forest walk. Let nature silence the cacophony of a screen-dependent world. Step away from the relentless race—where competition, overwork, and constant busyness take over—so you can reconnect with what truly matters. Being busy for the sake of being busy often masks deeper, unaddressed issues. Embrace stillness as often as possible. Life is not a race.

Free yourself from limiting beliefs, paralyzing fears, and the grip of past mistakes. These burdens weigh down your growth. By letting go, you lighten your load, creating space for an open-hearted self, ready to embrace life with renewed vigor. Moving forward doesn't require force or conformity to rigid molds. Instead, flow naturally toward opportunities aligned with your true potential. Each bold step—no matter how imperfect—takes you closer to the most empowered version of yourself. When satisfied with progress and content, take a break. Don't let perfect be the enemy of the good. No individual or situation is perfect. Being happy with what you've got is a good thing. Yet avoid complacency and execute incremental improvements in a measured fashion.

Face challenges with confidence and composure. Even mistakes such as taking the wrong job provide clarity about what you truly desire. Persevering through tough experiences reveals invaluable lessons about resilience and hard work.

It may not always feel ideal, but stepping outside your comfort zone builds character. With time, you'll come to appreciate even the things you once resisted. That's the nature of growth—it turns obstacles into opportunities and discomfort into strength. Sometimes a misstep will help you course-correct, guiding you toward a better-aligned next move. Every tough experience, from grueling shifts to unglamorous jobs, contributes to your story and growth. These experiences provide practical lessons and resilience that no textbook or classroom can teach. As the saying goes, "They don't teach that at Harvard Business School."

Relying on yourself during uncertain times fosters a deep inner strength that remains steadfast through future challenges. Whether you're working a midnight shift or navigating complex responsibilities, these trials shape your ability to adapt, persevere, and thrive. Over time, you'll see these struggles not as setbacks but as vital building blocks in the foundation of your character.

Looking back on life's hard lessons with gratitude reveals the power of perspective. The hustle, grit, and perseverance required to push through challenges are essential to your success. Live responsibly, honor your mission, and prioritize integrity in your decisions. Through trial and error, each step stretches your abilities, strengthens your resolve, and brings you closer to the life that's uniquely yours.

Embrace your truth with courage and determination—not anyone else's version of it. This thoughtful combination of effort, reflection, and ethical living delivers profound fulfillment. You will get what you focus on; manifest, then experience. In many ways, a belief held is simply a poor excuse for an experience. More profound is rather, walking the walk, where beliefs and ideas are only that!

CHALLENGING YOURSELF

SET AMBITIOUS GOALS AND WORK DILIGENTLY TO ACHIEVE THEM

Highly successful individuals consistently demonstrate remarkable abilities and efficiency across many spheres of life. Some excel with a structured to-do list of their own tasks, while others thrive in dynamic environments, seizing spontaneous opportunities through effective team communication—whether via group texts, social media, or public speaking engagements. Many leverage long-standing friendships and professional networks to accomplish their goals, recognizing the power of collaboration.

Achieving dreams begins with laser-focused goal setting and the proactive assembly of a strong, supportive team. Serial entrepreneurs are particularly noteworthy for their capacity to achieve what might typically require extensive resources and large teams. They tackle challenges with precision and unwavering focus, expertly dividing attention between current tasks and future strategic moves. Their foresight enables them to seamlessly transition from one venture to the next, optimizing their time and energy.

These entrepreneurs have a keen eye for recognizing the intrinsic value of investments, whether in real estate, stocks, or collectibles, and they cultivate well-diversified portfolios. This same skill extends to their management practices—they know when to sever ties with underperforming or dishonest consultants and team members. Their decision-making is guided by efficiency, an intolerance for wasted time, and an unwavering drive toward success.

The energy of a true winner is unmistakable—you can feel their presence even before they speak. It's *real*, dynamic, and alive. If this energy hasn't yet entered your life, the good news is that it can today. You have the power to choose it, to embrace that force within you. Trial and error. Start now with something small. And if you already experience this powerful energy, congratulations! You're on the right track.

Winners consistently communicate with enthusiasm and optimism. They use language like, "I'll take care of that right away," "What an amazing experience," and "She's an incredible athlete and a great asset to the community." Their words radiate positivity, always balanced by action that consistently moves them forward. The key to their success lies not in obsessing over failures, but in learning from them. For these individuals, each setback is a steppingstone, a data point for growth, one they don't hesitate to highlight as part of their success story. They stay focused on progress and rarely dwell on the past or regret the journey.

This raises an interesting question: why do so many artists seem happy despite not always having financial success? The answer lies in their pursuit of purpose. Being a struggling artist might seem difficult on the surface, but for those who follow their passion, it's often a deeply fulfilling life. They don't choose their path for material wealth but because it aligns with their soul's purpose. While capitalism often equates success with wealth and competition, many artists understand that true success isn't about winning at others' expense—it's about finding joy in the process and contributing something meaningful to the world. Too often, we measure success by money alone, but real happiness comes from connection, purpose, and fulfillment. If you die rich but have lived an empty, unfulfilled life, was it really worth it? True fulfillment comes from living with intention. So focus on what truly matters to you—whether it's your passions, your community, or your inner calling. Share your talents not just for personal gain, but for the collective good. What fills your soul? What excites you every day? That's where your energy belongs. You will love it.

What sets achievers apart is their discipline, diligence, and resilience. Much like dedicated athletes, they consistently show up and push forward, regardless of the obstacles. They embody a relentless drive to excel in all areas of life, approaching challenges with a no-excuses mindset.

A crucial component of their personal growth is self-reflection. Something as simple as a daily glance in the mirror can be a moment to affirm positivity and accountability. It's a practice of reinforcing that you are responsible for your progress—no one else. Own every aspect of your journey, from successes to setbacks, and move forward with intention.

Progress toward ambitious goals starts with small steps: trying new things, meeting new people, and putting yourself out there. These initial efforts build the foundation for bold leaps into opportunities that align with your passions and purpose. Whether in business or social endeavors, staying attuned to the feelings and excitement driving you ensures that your actions remain congruent with your greater intent. When aligned, yes, you will feel it.

The most successful individuals are masters of time and resource management. They live wisely, often within their means, while cultivating multiple income streams through side hustles, small businesses, and investments. They prioritize diversification, spreading wealth across avenues like stocks, ETFs, bonds, money markets, and real estate. Instead of indulging in frivolous luxuries, they invest in meaningful experiences and opportunities for future growth.

These go-getters build strong, trusted teams of professionals, basing decisions on data, research, and sound knowledge rather than fleeting trends. They understand that sustained effort, guided by passion and vision, ultimately overcomes any challenge. By embracing minimalist efficiency, they remove distractions to focus on what truly matters. This mindset helps them balance ambition with joy, finding fulfillment in the journey rather than solely chasing outcomes. It's this genuine passion and intentionality that set them on a path of long-term growth and success. Striking a balance is key. Thriving on chaos or multi-tasking is the cup of tea for many. Find yours.

Another essential element of success in achieving your goals is maintaining positive, focused self-talk throughout the day. Things may go wrong—especially in the morning—due to factors beyond your control. Don't let these setbacks define your day. Instead, push forward with resilience, avoiding negativity and frustration. Stay calm, remain level-headed, and take proactive steps to keep momentum moving in the right direction. How you choose to respond to challenges shapes your journey more than the challenges themselves.

Balance is key: carve out time for reading, exercising, eating well, and enjoying life. Work hard, play hard, and remain present for yourself and others. This equilibrium fuels progress, ensuring that you not only achieve success but also embrace the joy, purpose, and fulfillment that make the journey truly worthwhile. You can have it all: balance, good health yet unstoppable progress.

Continually Seek Self-Improvement

Are you working up to your full potential to create your own joy? It's crucial not to short-change yourself in life. This means maximizing your experiences, pushing yourself mentally and physically, and cultivating healthy thoughts that aren't tied to monetary rewards. Laugh often!

Whether you're breaking a sweat at the gym or challenging your intellect, approach each task with intensity. Set mental or written targets and deadlines. Without those, life can easily pass by without direction. Mediocrity can trap you, leaving you feeling aimless, like a ship adrift at sea. It's easy to settle for comfort or give up too soon. The key is to challenge yourself consistently, elevate your energy, and finish what you start. A year from now you'll be astounded by the results.

Many happy people love their craft so much that it feels like attending a party every day. Everything they do is lined up, front and center, with energy and enthusiasm for tackling each problem in sight, striving to reach their maximum potential. When this enthusiasm is combined with positive mindsets and the strength of a supportive team, amazing things happen. Passion, prolific ideas, clear goals, and a sense of selflessness make great things possible.

Setbacks don't stop high achievers; they are like steam locomotives full of positive energy, with backup plans ready if one fails. Problem-solving comes quickly, and even when facing challenges, there's no complaining. These individuals maintain a blend of assertiveness, humility, and a focus on helping their team members succeed. Remember: people come first, then money. Having this order prioritized for the right reasons fosters joy and fulfillment. As financial show host Suze Orman often reiterated, "It's people, then money, then things." In that order!

I once played basketball with a senior guy from a tech company who consistently passed the ball to others when he had possession. By the end of the game, he wasn't noticeably tired but had somehow managed to score the most points. He seemed to have the most fun and graciously congratulated the opposing team after our victory. Observing him, you could deduce a lot about him as a coworker. He played selflessly, wasted no energy, and showed kindness, humility, and composure. His communication was precise, with a no-nonsense, professional demeanor. He left with a firm handshake, embodying efficiency and balance. These qualities were easy to notice in just twenty minutes.

If someone were to emulate this man's behavior and mindset they could lead any company with success. However, those with big egos, who are self-centered, aloof, or lack self-awareness, could play alongside him and still miss the message. It's baffling that someone can miss the essence of a balanced, efficient, and humble person. But many people are too fixated on what they want to notice the true joy of life. It's often a form of ignorance, stubbornness, or selfishness. When confronted about what they've missed, their ego may block self-awareness, and they remain oblivious to their own opportunities for growth.

In The Peter Principle, authors Laurence J. Peter and Raymond Hull suggest that individuals are promoted to their level of incompetence, reaching a point where they plateau. While self-taught skills can help you advance, after you master a task there comes a time when new self-talk becomes necessary, guiding you toward growth and the next level.

Throughout this journey, it's vital for your mental and physical well-being to avoid burnout by not focusing too intensely on a single pursuit. Take breaks—switching from reading or studying to relaxing outside, enjoying a brisk walk, running errands, or taking a stroll by a placid lake. Tackling the day's most challenging tasks after breaks helps prevent monotony and rigidity, contributing to a healthier routine.

Achieving balance means blending work and play and investing time in relationships, hobbies, and side hustles. Understanding where and with whom your time is best spent is key. Tap into your analytical side—conduct a comparative analysis, run numbers, and research online. Before you know it, a clear plan will form. Envision the END result before you even start. Visualize a phenomenally great ending; But, will that truly make you happy? A house in the South of France will not make you happy if you're stuck in old thoughts, refusing to get out of your own way. Wherever you go, there you are. Do the interior work, address what your needs truly are, deep down. Resolve this ASAP, and it will save a lot of time, money and recurring frustration.

Don't forget to celebrate incremental wins. Achievements, however small, should be acknowledged. It's not just another day—it's progress by you, and these shifts mark meaningful improvement in your journey. Thanking others for their help will be both fulfilling and appreciated. Also, when forging ahead with progress, don't be concerned with being the protagonist of "shoot the messenger". Someone has to dive into the middle and mix it up to achieve progress. If you sit still complacently and you're not part of the solution, the problem will eat you alive. You become a target. Ask meaningful, direct questions and shake things up. The quicker you have answers the better.

6
ADDRESS SELF-SABOTAGE

Self-sabotage can prevent you from reaching your goals. Identify negative thoughts and behaviors, and adopt a flexible, adaptable approach to overcome them.

THIS CHAPTER COVERS:

Addressing Deep-Seated Thoughts and Feelings
- *Identify underlying issues that cause self-sabotage.*
- *Seek help if necessary to address deep-rooted problems.*

Overcoming Self-Sabotage
- *Develop positive habits that support your goals.*
- *Eliminate behaviors that hinder your progress.*

Flexibility for Change
- *Be open to changing your plans as needed.*
- *Adapt to new circumstances and opportunities.*

ADDRESSING DEEP-SEATED THOUGHTS AND FEELINGS

Identify Underlying Issues That Cause Self-Sabotage

We embody and live with the cumulative choices we've made—whether those choices were carefully curated or the result of hasty, thoughtless decisions. Life often becomes a series of major commitments, each consuming endless hours of work: deadlines, constant stress from every direction, and the pressure to please others. Yet, these commitments are typically ones we've chosen, scheduled, and initiated. So why don't we finish things or, said more bluntly, lie to ourselves?

Did success come too easily? Are we still weighed down by past mistakes, guilt, or stuck in the past? Even when we do the work, why do we struggle to accept or celebrate achievements?

Understanding the complex thoughts, feelings, and self-perceptions that lead to self-sabotage can be difficult, especially when we are sincerely pursuing a dream or a labor of love. Some people engage in activities simply for the enjoyment, the challenge, or the thrill of the experience. For them, the journey is all that matters; the end result, or whether credit is received, takes a back seat. For those who take this approach, it can be hard to see what drives them deep down, or how much they really care about specific goals. It's how it makes them feel—not raw results.

It's important, then, to look beyond the surface and explore what might be impeding your progress. Many things that might have flourished easily could have blossomed if met with joy, not hesitation. The behavior of halting just short of success—perhaps learned from a family member or rooted in a habitual fear of failure—can become a pattern that sabotages our efforts. It brings us back to the critical questions: Why are we doing this in the first place? What motivated our original intent and decision? Was it a genuine passion, or were we simply trying to stay busy, *look* successful, please others, or force ourselves into something we never truly loved in the first place?

This deeper reflection may require a great deal of introspection, maybe even the guidance of a skilled counselor to help unpack it. Sometimes, there's no quick solution to self-sabotage—only grit, self-discovery, and navigating those dark areas within us. The next step is a fresh start: resetting, adjusting, and reaching out for help when necessary.

Even if you don't feel that counseling is warranted, getting insight into our limiting beliefs and behaviors might need an outside perspective. We all perceive things uniquely, especially in relation to the expectations we set for ourselves. Sometimes speaking with a trusted friend can help dislodge limiting thought processes and clear the way. However, having the mind of a certified professional assist seems a winning option. By sharing, we not only open up our own perspective but recognize that others are navigating their own struggles. Uncertainty and anxiety are often fueled by self-imposed pressure, haste, and the overwhelming weight of expectations.

Consider self-sabotage an opportunity to tailor and adjust your approach, and allow yourself the grace to visualize the joy that will come from completing your revised goal. You owe it to yourself to address these issues, working through them thoughtfully. You deserve happiness and contentment.

Avoid labeling yourself negatively because of past disappointments—it's just another wasted pity party. Likewise, blaming others may offer temporary relief, but in the end, it's nothing more than a cycle of thoughts, expectations, and excuses bouncing around in your mind. When you adopt a negative label, you become trapped in that identity—it shapes your actions and limits your potential. But here's the truth: you can reset that label in an instant. Everything you touch can turn to gold if you simply open the door, manifest, visualize success, and *try*. Fearlessly move forward, building confidence with each step, each experience, and every moment of progress.

With intentionality—letting go of old labels, adjusting your attitude, practicing forgiveness—you can cultivate a new outlook and approach to life. This reset can help you live a richer, more fulfilling life. Leave the past where it belongs—in the past. Cling only to the good memories of your choice, letting go of failures, regrets, or pain. Otherwise, you run the risk of becoming your own worst enemy. Change your mindset and you will change your life. Don't limit your thinking—dream bigger than big, then go even further. It's not only okay to have it all, but also your birthright.

SEEK HELP IF NECESSARY TO ADDRESS DEEP-ROOTED PROBLEMS

While working alone on your craft can be appealing, there is great value in learning from others and their hundreds of ideas that you may love. Engaging conversations, shared experiences, and reassurance that you're not alone can help enrich your perspective. Your effort is compulsory.

When life feels overwhelming, don't bury yourself in the problem—seek help. Major accomplishments are rarely achieved alone. From landing on the moon to winning Olympic medals, every success story has a team behind it. There's no shame in asking for support. In fact, collaboration often makes the journey more enjoyable and effective than struggling in isolation. Many thrive in daily teamwork: a teacher learns from fellow educators and students, an artist or wealth manager gains insights from colleagues, and a finish carpenter exchanges ideas with a cabinet designer. Success is built through shared knowledge and connection—embrace it.

We form habits that often feel unchangeable, especially for those with stubborn personalities—people who insist on having things their way and refuse to compromise. What may seem laughable to some is, for them, all about control. The term *control freak* defines a way of life for many, often rooted in underlying insecurities or fear-based anxieties. When life feels unpredictable, they try to control what they *can*, frustrated by everything beyond their grasp. But this habit not only frustrates others—it also limits the person themselves, preventing them from exploring their true potential. Breaking free from rigid thinking starts with awareness. A good counselor can be invaluable in identifying negative thought patterns and limiting beliefs. The key is to avoid staying stuck—address your concerns, learn the lessons, and move forward. Don't dwell on obstacles; use them as steppingstones for growth.

As my favorite saying goes, *some people don't know what they don't know*. And each can be severely dangerous if not expensive on any given front. So, if you recognize what you *don't* know, you position yourself for long-term success—saving time, money, frustration, and mostly—embarrassment. Seek guidance from experts, build a strong support system, and take the next best step. That's exactly what I did throughout my career—I surrounded myself with experts. And wow, were they smart and impressive! Get advice from three trusted professionals, make an informed decision, then move forward. Most importantly, *thank them* for their help. Without them what would you have?

OVERCOMING SELF-SABOTAGE

Develop Positive Habits That Support Your Goals

Developing a mindset of dreaming big is fun and key to pursuing ambitious goals. Don't allow overthinking or negative self-talk to block your path. Feed yourself with positive thoughts and affirmations, focusing on what's possible rather than what's holding you back. Stay attuned to opportunities and take calculated risks that will propel you toward growth and stability. Every small step adds momentum toward your dreams.

One amazingly powerful way to cultivate positivity throughout your workday is by surrounding yourself with reminders of past achievements or loved ones. These small tokens serve as anchors, grounding you in a positive mindset. The more you do this, the more this positivity becomes embedded within you. As challenges arise, you'll find yourself responding with confidence, guided by the positive habits you've built into your daily routine. And one day, you might even laugh at your younger self—the version of you that once thought they had it all figured out. Take a moment to reflect on that. Growth comes from humility, from realizing that learning never stops. Honesty is the best policy—especially with yourself. Don't fall into the trap of self-deception. Isn't that a refreshing thought?

Take a moment each day to reflect: *What brought you the most happiness today?* Write it down, celebrate it, and aim to repeat it. Notice the small changes in your routine that make you feel your best and incorporate them regularly. These little shifts build lasting positive habits. Now, ask yourself: *How am I feeling in this very moment?* If there's any discontent, what's the next step—will you stew in it or take action? That's always the real question. And the truth is, nobody can do it for you but *you*.

Physical exercise plays an invaluable role in this process. It clears your mind and elevates your mental state. Exercising with intensity strengthens not only your body but also your mind, making it easier to combat negative thinking and vulnerability. Exercise fortifies your physical being and pulls you out of a cycle of worry and guilt. If exercise is not currently part of your routine, adding a few simple workouts a week will reap big dividends. Similarly, good sleep habits and a healthy diet will support your mind and body as you work toward your goals. Adhere to a schedule!

You are the director of your own thoughts. You have the power to choose which ones to entertain and which to discard. With intentional effort, you can cultivate thoughts that empower, uplift, and energize you. Embrace every positive moment, thrive in the present, and let those good feelings elevate every aspect of your life. Ever wonder why a few of your friends always seem to be in a good mood? Maybe they've been to hell and back—but they still smile at you, still hug you. So, who's going to be the bigger person? Who will rise above complaints and negativity? That's the real test. That's the choice.

Eliminate Behaviors That Hinder Your Progress

Avoid wasting your limited time on pointless behaviors like comparing, catastrophizing, overanalyzing, and avoiding. Instead, face everything head-on. Get centered, and enthusiastically uplift those around you. Think about how you feel when others compliment, support, or encourage you. Now, it's your turn to do the same! Comparing yourself to others is a losing game. Your mission is to become the unique version of yourself that you were meant to be. When you do compare, let it be with your own personal best—never with others. Others may inspire you, but ultimately, you are your own measure of success.

Stay in control of your actions and decisions. Fear is one of the biggest obstacles to progress—it breeds excuses, fuels indecision, and makes life unpleasant for those around you. But here's the truth: fear is nothing more than a creation of your imagination, especially when it comes to an unpredictable future. Letting fear dictate your choices leads to stagnation, filling your path with stop signs and hesitation. But remember, we are not promised tomorrow—*action* is what brings fulfillment. Stop dwelling on past hardships. Instead, take a few steps today toward building a new reality—one filled with victories and achievements. Shift your mindset to one of happiness, success, growth, and *trying*. Because progress starts the moment you decide to move forward.

Identify and address your mental hang-ups—those issues that lead to *paralysis by analysis* and halt your progress. It's easy to deceive yourself, clouding your judgment and finding excuses to procrastinate when you're unmotivated. Recognize these patterns and push through them; you'll feel better on the other side.

Think about the last time you avoided something important—perhaps earlier today when your significant other asked a crucial relationship question. Did you defer the conversation? Avoidance only escalates concerns, creating roadblocks that guarantee issues will not go away. Delaying action allows problems to fester. Address these matters now, regardless of the speed bumps they may create. Doing so will free up your energy and allow you to make meaningful progress toward your goals. Remember, no one is perfect; it's all about how you choose to react, listen, and adjust—with heartfelt compassion.

FLEXIBILITY FOR CHANGE

BE OPEN TO CHANGING YOUR PLANS AS NEEDED

It can be challenging to recognize the defense mechanisms we build to protect ourselves. If you find yourself resisting change, it might be because you believe change is impossible. The key is to loosen your grip and consider how flexible you need to be to embrace change.

Ultimately, change benefits the mind, body, and spirit. So why not embrace it? Be open enough to explore options that bring you happiness. The alternative is stagnation—maintaining the status quo and resigning yourself to the belief that things can't change without effort.

Yes, it requires effort and energy to change, but the rewards are worth it. If you find a partner or family member draining your energy, address it calmly and directly. Treat the situation as a puzzle to solve together, working as a team. Ask questions rather than anger or unfounded accusations. Compromise and negotiate, as life is not one-sided or about solely fulfilling your own desires. Solutions often emerge once you move out of your own way, and paying close attention to others' thoughts is crucial in finding mutual understanding. Keep things practical rather than emotional. Ultimately, believe that change is possible. Maybe they just need a hug or feel unsupported.

The result may be far removed from your initial mental snapshot. In retrospect, you may laugh at your initial expectations and off-base perspective. Learn as you go; don't beat yourself up when encountering obstacles or making mistakes. Don't be embarrassed to ask for help, and don't wait until the last second.

Creating a new life plan is about enjoying the journey, not just the destination. Embrace both the good and the bad. The challenges—failures, unmet expectations, disagreements—often provide the best lessons. Use compassion as your guide; helping others matters more than profits, checklists, or feeding endless egos.

It's easy to get off track or become unbalanced, swinging between negativity and over-optimism, or rushing through steps that require careful attention. Avoid cutting corners or believing every thought that crosses your mind. Your self-talk can easily derail your plans if you're not consistently reflecting and making necessary adjustments.

Stay focused on your intentions and specific goals. Ask yourself: *What was my goal, and where am I now on that path?* And remember to finish—always! In the end, you'll feel accomplished for making each decision. There's no such thing as a free lunch; you must put in the work and make it happen.

Adapt to New Circumstances and Opportunities

Ground yourself in the truth of your situation on a daily basis. Be realistic, acknowledging both the positive and negative elements of each decision you make. Understand your personal limits and boundaries. Stay within your comfort zone until you feel safe and are ready to take calculated risks. Manage expectations and recognize what you and others can tolerate. When offered a new opportunity, ask questions—digging, prying relentlessly, uncovering every detail. Don't make any decision until you reach a comfort level that suits you. You'll know when you do, you can just feel it.

Sometimes, it's the basics that must change—things like money. Analyze your budget a couple of times per month. If something is reducing your returns, like overspending or overcharges, dig deep for specifics. Determine what value is not supporting your goal. Can you cut any costs? Locate extra funds unnecessarily spent. Can you afford to go out to lunch every day, or should you bring your lunch instead? Decide where to trim so you can run a leaner, more aggressive accounting sheet. Spend time reflecting on your preferences and priorities. Explore the problems that come with each complication, interrogating any resistance you feel from stepping outside your comfort zone. Address anything that feels unsettling, then move on.

To gain clarity, find a quiet room and take a moment to look outside at the glorious, ever-changing sky. A cleared mind, fully present in each moment, is a treasured gift you give to yourself. Identify your happy place and visit it as often as possible. Whether it's sitting in a peaceful garden or offering a kind word to a homeless person, remember that the best things in life are free.

Recharge and reset, then send your positive energy out into the universe. Each of these small steps can have a profound impact on your refreshed mindset.

7
DEFINE AND ACHIEVE SUCCESS

Success is personal and unique to each individual. Define what success means to you and prioritize your goals accordingly, without comparing yourself to others.

THIS CHAPTER COVERS:
———————————

Defining Success
- *Create your own definition of success based on your values and aspirations.*
- *Focus on what truly matters to you.*

Prioritizing Personal Goals
- *Identify your top priorities and allocate time and resources accordingly.*

Avoiding Comparisons
- *Refrain from comparing yourself to others.*
- *Celebrate your achievements and progress.*

DEFINING SUCCESS

CREATE YOUR OWN DEFINITION OF SUCCESS BASED ON YOUR VALUES AND ASPIRATIONS

Embarking on a journey to discover your authentic self leads to the gradual unveiling of what truly holds meaning for you—what you deeply want and desire. Initially, this might feel like short-term survival mode, but eventually, it transforms into a process of understanding long-term needs and dreams—aspects of life that only you can define. Living according to others' goals and desires often leads to a lingering sense of longing or emptiness. When you design **yours**, you get to own it.

Think outside the box and try something new each week. Plan your goals for the next week and month in manageable increments. Many great minds suggest reading extensively; even just twenty minutes of reading in the morning and at sunset can generate fresh ideas every day.

Never ignore your gut instincts or inner motivations, as they are the driving force toward your true path. The mantra "fake it 'til you make it" is some of the worst advice out there. Pretending to be something you're not and building a fabricated, inauthentic life only leads you further away from your true self—the unique individual the universe has created. Ultimately, it's a lie you tell yourself that distorts your journey of self-discovery.

By staying true to your values and integrity, you ensure that your decisions align with your deeper sense of self. Whether you're moving forward with something or choosing to walk away from a situation, knowing why and when to act makes all the difference.

Deciding to end or elevate something—whether it's ending a business relationship, shifting career paths, or investing in your personal or financial well-being—requires thoughtful consideration of your ethics, expectations, and personal goals. Your code of ethics forms the foundation for your decisions, guiding you toward choices that support both your peace of mind and long-term success. Ultimately, the way you approach your work, relationships, and future should align with your vision for the life you want to create. This alignment helps you stay on track with your personal and financial goals while preserving your inner well-being. By taking a proactive and thoughtful approach, you ensure that every decision is made with purpose, clarity, and confidence.

Narrowing down a defined purpose with clarity sets you up for success. The feelings you experience upon delivering something purely from within yourself, uninfluenced by others, yield high dividends on many fronts. It feels good, visceral, worth the true effort; a resonating feeling abounds. That which is well thought out, drawn from experience and wisdom and from your honest thoughts, lets your essence ring true. Be guided by everything aligned with your belief system, ethics, goodwill, and intentions—from your soul, not your best friend's or your coworker's. Considering others' input can be valuable, collectively and cumulatively; yet it's your true desires, long-term goals, and passions that ultimately hit the mark. It must come from you.

When our minds derail, they tend to wander—like endless rabbit holes in an ever-distracting internet search. Stay focused. Create a daily schedule, but you must stick to it; taking small, consistent steps toward both short- and long-term goals. This discipline keeps you on track; without it, it's easy to drift aimlessly. Stay the course, and you'll feel the magic unfold from deep within. Progress comes full circle, especially when you radiate inspiring energy—spreading peace, love, and joy. Good karma flows effortlessly when love and honesty shine through in every direction.

This takes me to music, where you can feel it deep down—gifted singers transmitting intense emotions of positivity, love, and vibrational energy. Music, much like karma, can be a source of inspiration, offering lyrical ideas to explore, question, and reflect upon. For musicians, particularly those who aren't celebrities, there's a special kind of appreciation for the work itself. It's fulfilling when one soul enjoys a song, but even more rewarding is creating it for yourself, to your own standards.

My album *Send Them Love* was crafted from pure love for music. While I was writing the lyrics, an elderly woman in a New Mexico farming museum said to me, "Send them love." Her words resonated deeply with the true intent of the album's lyrics. When I first began writing and recording the album, I couldn't predict the outcome. Each turn was shrouded in mystery, yet every note, lyric, and creative choice radiated positive energy. The process felt like a stream of consciousness, a divine intervention weaving its way through—a work of art revealing itself. We're all here for a purpose, so listen to the whispers. Revelations abound when you open the doors. The universe supports all that you desire, but you must do the work and take action.

Artistic expression isn't confined to a set definition. The intent behind the work, however, must be clear. When art is done from the heart, for the right reasons, it gives rise to harmonious honesty, igniting a chain of good energy. It's like a pottery wheel spinning at its sweet spot, smooth and unshaken—your path naturally unfolds, setting everything into motion fluidly and prolifically.

Your quest requires digging and scraping to the bottom of your most intimate feelings and soul; reaching the embedded roots of your belief system to discover what sparks your passion and fuels your motivation. Proceed when things begin to feel right, BUT after, and only after, you're happy with the entire game plan. Go with your gut instincts, your inner sanctum, and again the soft whisper in the back of your mind. Listen closely: it is there!

Defining purpose in team projects means digging deep as well—with yourself and with team members. If you have a target for your team, proceed cautiously, confirm the mission; ask direct, innocuous questions before you're underway. If your team boasts a vociferous opponent of an agreed scope, take stock and heed their advice. This unbashful soul may have saved you lots of time, money, and effort, if not all three.

Focus on What Truly Matters to You

Follow pursuits that align with your personal values. Listen to your instincts. If something lacks meaning or fails to enrich you, you'll feel empty at day's end. Be selective and focused when investing your time. Engaging in meaningless pursuits that divert from your goals is a disservice to yourself. Keep the energy vampires at bay! That which is genuine and authentic, the true you, must be identified to set your course for a fresh start. This requires brutal honesty as to what you believe in, what makes you tick and truly resonates. The more honesty the more time saved.

I feel an amassed energy of fullness when I've had eclectic days filled with progress on a variety of tasks, such as looked for a deal on land to buy, weighed out an investment property, bought a few affordable long-term stocks, helped elderly neighbor, exercised, supported friends who've fallen on hard times, checked out five books, dreamt up an overseas trip, ate healthily, journaled, supported other artists' ventures, began drafting a new book and album song list. By mixing the day up, your mind can get excited by new frontiers—you make your own fun!

When you're feeling uncertain about whether a pursuit will enrich your life, make a list of pros and cons to aid in decision-making. Doing so will let you see clearly whether the cons go against your personal values and will also give you a sense of how much time and energy this pursuit will require.

Knowing your love language and that of others can also help you focus on what matters.

PRIORITIZING PERSONAL GOALS

IDENTIFY YOUR TOP PRIORITIES AND ALLOCATE TIME AND RESOURCES ACCORDINGLY

As university professor and pilot Scott Hudson often said, "Making decisions, prioritizing, and doing what feels right involves not just what is important, but what is MOST important to you." We all seek happiness, yet we define it differently, and many never reach their nirvana. It's essential to determine our limits and boundaries, both professionally and personally—specifically, what we can and cannot handle. We all have limits, pet peeves, idiosyncrasies, moods, and unrealistic expectations. Success means different things to different people, and it's often an overused term. Some may choose to simply "get by" in life.

Consider the mindset that allowed thousands of Olympic athletes to compete or what it takes for a musician to perform on stage, or for a young artist to exhibit oil paintings in Paris. Remember, thinking big is free. Not everyone wants to set the world on fire, compete professionally, or take a leap of faith—and that's perfectly okay. It's your prerogative to set goals or not. Whether you choose to take action or remain still, life will give you what you allow and withstand—based on your expectations, desires, and, most importantly, your ability to say "no" when necessary.

This is always your call. If you find yourself tossing around an idea in your mind and red flags keep popping up, believe what you see people do, not what you're told to think. Observe closely: watch for bad habits, recurring excuses, inflated optimism, and big talkers. Discern, deduce, analyze, and decide! Let's call this DDAD. Alternatively, mull, methodical, optimize, mitigate—let's call that MMOM.

I once saw a plaque quote on an uncle's wall, "I never had a bad day." Bravo—he must have loved his job. It's a bold but uplifting mindset to live by. Those words are powerful and help shape how we view each day. You become what you think. "I'm so blessed, my cup runneth over, today is another unbelievably great day." Repeat that three times—did it shift something for you? You decide your chosen approach and attitude. Always begin a new project or endeavor saying to yourself, "This is going to be easy and fun". No matter the size. Watch how your outlook changes. What you thought was gigantic becomes small, and problems are easily surmountable.

It's all about what you tell yourself. You're in charge of the tape recorder in your head. It's incredibly important to monitor it as you spearhead change in your life.

AVOIDING COMPARISONS

Refrain from Comparing Yourself to Others

If an artist creates a body of work solely for popularity, rather than from the heart or from their true visceral feelings, it can become the destruction of art. Understand your true beliefs; your values, priorities, intent, and those you trust. These elements are all crucial in propelling you to the next level. Assemble a meaningful package, truly representing your aspirations, with an aligned and heartfelt mission of truthful intent.

Think for yourself; it's absolutely crucial! Do you know someone who, when asked a tough question, turns to their partner and asks, "What do you think?" Refusing to stand for anything is a significant issue and, on some level, it's unfortunate. Whether your car has broken down on the side of the road, you're walking alone in the streets, or you're leaving a relationship, the ability and confidence to stand on your own two feet and think for yourself can never be overstated. It saves you time, stress, money, and confusion.

Many souls working in systematized corporate jobs—perhaps feeling confined to a cubicle—become so trapped in a non-free-thinking environment that they forget how to spread their wings and fly. Choices abound, so know yourself and recognize what makes you feel claustrophobic versus what makes you feel like the sky is the limit. Lean toward what makes you say, "I'm doing everything I love, every day!"

Be a leader, not a mindless, insecure follower of trends. Let's take a humorous but real detour: if you're constantly imitating others and jumping on societal trends, you're no longer being true to yourself. Let's say you want to feel validated and good about who you are—so maybe you copy someone else's tattoo, man-bun, or earring combo. Maybe you throw around phrases like "I'll circle back later … when I have the bandwidth." Maybe you even replicate their trendy car or mustache or adopt the empty sayings, "It is what it is" or "super [this], super [that]."

But by doing so, you've essentially signed up to be an actor—losing your authenticity. It's essentially a "stamped-out person," as if factory-made to fit in and gain acceptance or validation. In this example, very little is actual, real, or YOU. Instead of being yourself, you've morphed into a bland version of everything that's trendy, shallow, and insecure. Every athlete with a full arm of colorful tattoos now all look alike, forever inked.

- Your presence, your goals, and your life should represent the real you. The sooner you focus on what truly matters to that real you, the better your life will evolve. If you imitate friends, mimic heroes, or pursue goals set by others, you'll lose sight of your true self and your intended purpose on earth. Keeping up with trends, engaging in conversations to please others, rather than expressing your truth, are inauthentic and wasteful; on some level, they're a dishonest means of representing yourself. Gradually these behaviors will trap you in a mix of others' thoughts, goals, motives, aspirations, none truly reflecting you. Instead, a plastic AI robot. The unique and prolific Bob Dylan, Madonna, Elizabeth Taylor, Marlon Brando, Elvis, Joni Mitchell, Shane MacGowan of Pogues fame—refreshingly and seemingly copied no one. Watch any interview and learn from their individuality.

A few more things to ponder:

- When the chips are down, how many people stick around when you're facing challenges, hitting a wall, or going through tough times? The answer is usually zero—or maybe one. It's as if you have a contagious disease, like the dark vibes of a recent divorce or some other misfortune. They vanish with unparalleled speed, not wanting to be associated with your temporary struggles. But when you're winning, wealthy, accomplished, and supported by family or finances, it's a whole new ball game. In the end, your calm, self-confidence, growing skill set, additional education, and investment in yourself will pull you through. Keep it simple, stay grounded, lay the foundation, tell the truth, and know who you are.

- Let's delve into 'give and take': Why is it that when you give someone something for free, it holds no value? It could be a four-star dinner or an entire college education—received with zero gratitude—or countless other things I won't list here to spare you the frustration. They think you owe it to them, even though you were the one who worked for it. You treated them the way you'd want to be treated, but they wouldn't do the same for you. Why? Because not everyone has a giving heart. Many people are users, happy to take all they can get. That's why you need to stay on guard against freeloaders. You could be doing all the work while a manipulative soul sits back, feigning hardship with a daily pity party of aches, pains, and complaints. Assess the situation, and if necessary, disconnect—especially if it means protecting your own lifestyle. If you need to walk away, do it.

- Why does the old adage "honesty is the best policy" clear the deck and open up the skies? How many lies does the average person tell each day, and how many 'authors' on the internet are one hundred percent verified/correct in their writings? Most people lie to fit in, seek validation, or impress others—and that's not even counting the small embellishments. Worse, we often lie to ourselves, replaying false narratives like a broken record. This topic could be an entire book. Try this: commit to being completely truthful for a full week and watch how everything shifts. Fake friends will disappear. Your diet will improve. That flight to Asia you've been dreaming of? It gets booked. Freeloaders will stop taking advantage of you. Fantasies will turn into reality. You'll find a job you love instead of staying stuck in one you despise. You'll say "no" more often and no longer be a doormat. Best of all, the days of feeling sorry for yourself will be over. Honesty is free, while self-deception is like sucking canal water. Get real. Stop lying to yourself today and observe how the picture changes, whether it takes 10 days or 10 months. You don't need to be Mr. or Mrs. Agreeable all the time. Stop pleasing everyone else at your own expense.

- Why do hurt people hurt people? Unresolved pain and deep insecurities lash out like an out-of-control locomotive, lacking self-awareness and self-restraint, leaving destruction in their wake and wasting everyone's time. But when you truly know yourself, you become a solid rock, ready to face obstacles and challenges, even those presented by unfortunate souls.

- I recently heard a psychiatrist on a podcast say, "A child not embraced by the village will eventually burn it down to feel the warmth." There is so much packed into those words, the social and psychological implications. It's a searing yet profoundly accurate statement that cuts deep. The disconnect and isolation following COVID, the numbing rabbit holes of iPhones, and the prevalence of undiagnosed mental illness—what have we become in the aftermath of this technological tsunami? Loneliness and isolation have reached unprecedented levels, and the need for genuine human connection has never been more urgent in the history of our world.

Celebrate Your Achievements and Progress

It's necessary to take time out and rejoice in achieving milestones. So much is taken for granted in life. We are constantly bombarded by media nonsense and lightning-speed internet news, and its insanity becomes overwhelming. Meditate on a mountaintop, in the forest, or in a quiet room. Any space can become sacred if designated as such. Do whatever it takes to clear your mind and celebrate moments in your life. Celebrations, even small ones, hold great importance. Reaching a milestone is truly remarkable, especially one you have wholeheartedly pursued for the right reasons, driven by sheer passion.

Always be grateful for your success, if you cannot, something is certainly amiss. Reflect upon your past: have you failed to credit yourself for many amazing or selfless things you've accomplished? What do you deem a huge achievement? Is the metric monetary accumulation or helping others? Are you taking milestones for granted, barreling through life as if you're a locomotive? It's the small victories and baby steps of progress that begin humbly yet become huge one day.

Be grateful for all things: good or bad, big or small. Rarely feeling joy or giving yourself a pat on the back gives you little gratification from true progress. If you are experiencing significant success, yet still feel unfulfilled or dissatisfied, you need to question this. It was **you** who made it happen, so logically you should feel great. Maybe it's well-deserved credit for having met incremental goals. You have the power to decide what's a victory or a loss, progress or a waste of time.

Even our failures should be celebrated as a pathway to progress. We learn more from failure than we do from success and its comfort. Failure often exposes others' true colors, revealing who is genuine and who isn't. Unfortunately, some people change for the worse, especially when money is at stake.

Don't forget to lift your spirits with laughter, even in the face of failure, and credit yourself for at least trying. We all fail many times, but in the end, humor is a powerful medicine. It helps maintain balance and reminds us that not taking ourselves too seriously is essential. And if you see failures and setbacks as necessary components of success, you can see the humor in them more easily and celebrate them more authentically.

If you're feeling sad, go help someone who has it worse; that gesture will lift you up. A childhood friend who became a teacher had a father who always said to her, "Don't stay there and keep a clean house all day, running room to room, go out and help someone. Teach them to read, walk in the park, just do your best to help them out." In other words, people with problems need you more than the kitchen needs to be sparkly clean. To me, that was such powerful and selfless advice to give.

8
MANAGE TIME EFFECTIVELY

Effective time management is essential for productivity. Avoid distractions and time-wasting activities so you can focus on what truly matters.

THIS CHAPTER COVERS:

Judicious Time Management
- *Plan your day and stick to a schedule.*
- *Prioritize tasks based on importance and urgency.*

Avoiding Negative Influences
- *Identify and eliminate activities that waste your time.*
- *Surround yourself with productive and positive influences.*

Disengaging from Social Media
- *Limit social media use to essential interactions.*
- *Focus on real-life connections and activities.*

JUDICIOUS TIME MANAGEMENT

PLAN YOUR DAY AND STICK TO A SCHEDULE

A concentrated, defined focus is essential to succeeding, and this focus must be applied to your daily schedule. Once you've meticulously mapped out goals and dreams and aligned them with realistic expectations, it's the unwavering commitment to action that keeps you on track. Always have a few targets lined up to execute. Multitask, proceeding slowly at first and acknowledging what feels right. Add more to your plate as you go.

Do people who are constantly rushing ever truly accomplish anything meaningful? Rushing through life inevitably comes at a cost—whether it's quality, focus, or peace of mind. It's a recipe for burnout, an accident waiting to happen. Instead, decide who you want to be and move forward with intention—slowly, methodically, and calmly. A frantic pace will only drain you. You'll be so consumed with being busy that it'll feel like your head is about to spin off.

Start by creating a daily schedule that helps you prioritize tasks and manage your time more efficiently. This gives you control over your day, enabling you to shift your focus with ease. Take breaks to refresh your mind, stay on track, and avoid distractions. Scheduling your plan for tomorrow and sticking to it helps you focus on clear objectives. If you're more productive at night, create a prioritized to-do list the evening before. This allows for a smooth and focused start the next day. Clearing your inbox and handling texts in the evening sets the stage for a relaxed morning. The key is to find what works for you. For example, if morning meditation or yoga at six a.m. feels best, tackle administrative tasks the night before to avoid a stressful start.

Example of a Free Day, Weekend—Create your own list!
6 am Meditation – 7 am Healthy breakfast – 8 am Read newspapers – 9 am Exercise/stretch – 10 am Coffee with entrepreneur

– 11 am Reading – Noon Lunch – 1 pm Review investments – 2 pm Check on ill friend – 3 pm Lakeside yoga – 4 pm Sports event – 5 pm Dinner prep – 6 pm Internet business search – 7 pm Play piano – 8 pm Watch documentary – 9 pm Brainstorm new business ideas, contact list – 10 pm Read fiction.

A documentary about legendary artist Georgia O'Keeffe noted how she would rise early, wash up, and sit facing the rural New Mexico sunrise. When her long hair had dried, she'd begin her day, eating from her organic garden, surrounded by the stunning adobe architecture of her home. O'Keeffe, who lived to ninety-eight, created her own sanctuary, with expansive windows and breathtaking views of the mountains. Her paintings—depicting the landscapes she loved—are now showcased in museums worldwide, forever to inspire generations. O'Keeffe lived life on her own terms, true to herself. A full life well lived.

Making your commitments public can help you stay focused and accountable. For example, when I started writing lyrics for ten songs, I first chose a theme or album title. Then, I created ten song titles and publicly announced the album's release date—to my publicist and on social media. This commitment pushed me into action mode. I had backed myself into a corner, leaving no room for hesitation, cancellation, or procrastination. The press releases became a driving force, compelling me to execute quickly and efficiently. The only option was to keep the momentum going. For this book, I brainstormed 23 Chapter titles one Friday night. Forcing action.

PRIORITIZE TASKS BASED ON IMPORTANCE AND URGENCY

There will always be urgent tasks, and they can take up your whole day if you let them. Judiciously decide where your time is best spent. Take a deep breath, close your eyes, and ask yourself: *Is what I'm doing right now getting me toward my goals, or is it something else?* Reflect on this. Take breaks whenever needed to clear your mind, and distance yourself from anything or anyone that feels inauthentic or draining. Better choices are always ahead.

Learn to distinguish between the urgent and the important. Important tasks are ones that move you forward toward your goals. Urgent tasks are often related to other people's deadlines or requirements. If you've made a commitment then deliver, but don't let someone else's sense of urgency derail your day. Allocate blocks of time early in the day to make sure that your important tasks get the attention they require.

Sometimes, an important task is more complicated than you might have planned for and aspects of it can become urgent—for example, responding to emails, meeting application deadlines, and other time-sensitive tasks. Leave a buffer in each day to respond to urgent needs in a timely way.

AVOIDING NEGATIVE INFLUENCES

Identify and Eliminate Activities That Waste Your Time

Wasted time, much like empty conversations, is akin to excessive TV watching. The internet's endless distractions lead you down rabbit holes, steering you away from your personal goals. Successful, proactive individuals don't waste their mornings on TV or the internet. Instead, they read, enjoy a healthy breakfast, and get some exercise. Substituting TV and social media with reading books or writing poetry fosters growth and mindfulness. Think about the progress you've made in past years—was it based on watching endless commercials or the talking heads of late-night shows? Such distractions are huge time-killers. Anything you might miss will eventually appear in online updates or notifications, keeping you in the loop without wasting precious time.

Wasted time in traffic can be minimized by carpooling, listening to productive podcasts, or even moving closer to your job. If you own property, consider renting it out and living closer to work, boosting both your home's asset value and your rental income. If possible, add more rental properties every couple of years and have a professional manage them to reduce your workload.

If your workplace coffee station turns into a gossip hub, take your coffee elsewhere. Avoid meaningless chatter and toxic environments that drain your energy. After parting ways with such influences, let go of that negativity and don't look back. Hanging around those who only bring you down will pull you under. Never be rude, just avoid empty discussions and behaviors that lead nowhere.

Reflect: could you have contributed to a current problem by needing to own it all? If so, take responsibility and gradually step away from it. Identify when it's time to walk away from situations or habits that aren't yielding results. Trust your instincts—recognize when things are out of sync, learn from your mistakes, and embrace the growth that comes from the process of elimination. That's where progress and success come from, not from avoiding failure.

Accept that you are in a place in life because what happened needed to happen, clearing the way for new growth. Your good karma sent out is rotating back to you ten times bigger, occasionally amidst miracles. And isn't everything perfect when the dark clouds that were completely out of your control clear away to reveal gorgeous blue skies? It's because you kept chipping away, kept your head down with focus, took on the hard days that you didn't want to face.

Nobody goes through this life unscathed. Hold steady; you're not alone. Run your own game, know who you are, and never look back. As an Instagram fave stated, "you become a badass &^%%&* when you decide what you're going to react to." Thus:

Set your bar higher than high and set the naysayers to the side. The only person in your way is you and the silly creation of *self-talk excuses*. Avoid being jealous or insecure. Others are not your competition; to the contrary, they show you what else can be done, so team up and learn from the best.

Surround Yourself with Productive and Positive Influences

I've met many entrepreneurs whose positivity is so powerful that they view negativity as something akin to a disease. They struggle to know how to deal with negative individuals because their focus, optimism, and upbeat attitude are their default state. For them, negativity feels foreign and indigestible, disrupting their otherwise constructive self-talk and way of life. A pessimist encountering such a can-do soul may be blindsided, almost like running into a brick wall.

Once, I was watching a parade of protesters marching down the downtown mall in my town, alongside a hugely successful entrepreneur—someone on fire with optimism. As we observed the scene, I had to explain their complaints to him. He kept shaking his head in disbelief, as if I had transported him to Mars and shown him Martians. Having grown up earning every penny on his own, he was completely self-sufficient, much like me. To his trained mindset and intense work ethic, their actions and expectations were baffling, if not depressing.

And yet, despite his initial reaction, he found beauty in their outfits, offering them compliments as he consciously shook off any negative energy. His body language and outlook revealed a different kind of wiring—he instinctively associated their protest with failure or a broken system. Perhaps they had a valid point, and maybe he was too quick to judge, but he would have none of it.

Many entrepreneurs start with a stable foundation: supportive, balanced parents who offer encouragement without being overbearing. These parents, who guide with a *challenge-yourself* attitude, foster success. Others rise to success on their own, driven by an internal force, without help from their parents. Some embrace constructive criticism, shaping it into their personal success formula, while others rebel before figuring things out on their own.

When you're faced with negativity, shift the conversation towards something positive or inspiring. Ask about others, change the subject, remove yourself from toxic situations right away. We can't change others, yet we can choose where to invest our time and energy. Deciding whom and what to focus on—those who truly support you—is crucial. It's a muscle strengthened with practice. To win the day, choose who belongs on your "team bus."

Being an astute listener is indispensable. You'll become cognizant that misinterpreted facts or beliefs are clarified when you hear both sides of a dispute. When naysayers or negative people enter the equation, do the right thing, do the hard work, and take the high road. Don't waste time with folks full of hot air who enjoy hearing themselves talk but add no value.

DISENGAGING FROM SOCIAL MEDIA

Limit Social Media Use to Essential Interactions

Social media has many people addicted to scrolling and texting nonstop, rather than fully living and enjoying life as it unfolds. It often signals a vacuous existence, an attempt to fill emptiness with busy work, or a lack of imagination.

Reflect on your own use of social media. Is it truly pursuing your dreams? Social media can create a parallel universe, but could 1,000 hours spent scrolling have been used to write two or three books? Disengage from following the crowd—stand out and think for yourself. Take charge of something, even if it's small, and embrace responsibility. Leadership and persistence build confidence. Mistakes and corrections are key to growth.

Social media networking has its value, but face-to-face interactions—conferences, music shows, art exhibitions, and other gatherings—can lead to much more meaningful connections. These moments offer valuable insights, tips, and opportunities that reinforce and align with your true needs.

Focus on Real-Life Connections and Activities

Online courses and Zoom groups facilitate connections, but nothing surpasses human interaction, the spoken word, and physical touch. Investing in yourself through engaging in real-life activities cultivates maturity, versatility, and heightened skills akin to those of the Renaissance souls we all admire. Action is key.

When you're engaging in activities listen closely to others, embodying a can-do spirit, always seeking possibilities. Confidently walk away from anything that doesn't feel right or balanced, practicing the valuable skill of saying 'no.' Surround yourself with goal-oriented individuals whose positive mindsets fuel success. Face-to-face conversations not only bring life to others but also offer a chance to better understand potential collaborators. While technology—email and texting—has shifted social dynamics, it can also lead to miscommunication.

Each step you take, whether forging new friendships, joining clubs, engaging in athletics, or starting a group, represents an investment in yourself, reflecting your varied interests and fostering your self-expression.

9
CLEAR OUT NEGATIVITY

Removing negative influences from your life is crucial for personal growth. Start fresh and concentrate on positive, fulfilling activities and relationships.

THIS CHAPTER COVERS:

Resetting and Starting Fresh
- Let go of past mistakes and start anew.
- Embrace new opportunities with a positive mindset.

Streamlining Operations
- Simplify your life by eliminating unnecessary tasks and commitments.
- Align your priorities with your core values.

Avoiding Unsatisfactory Partnerships
- Evaluate potential collaborators by starting small.
- End relationships and partnerships that drain your energy.
- Seek out positive and supportive connections.

RESETTING AND STARTING FRESH

LET GO OF PAST MISTAKES AND START ANEW

Do you find yourself burdened by guilt from childhood experiences or unforgiven mistakes from the deep dark past? Are you a pleaser, sometimes feeling like a doormat, overly fatigued, not fighting back? Is a voice in the back of the mind, repeating itself, haunting you at times? It's understandably exhausting. Why do we dwell on or relive unpleasant, unhappy times?

Learning how to say no is crucial. Move on from the past and let go of any confusion entangled in your mind. The past cannot be changed. You can release the past in an instant; forgiving others is a gift to yourself. Certain things you may deem unforgivable; perhaps you'll decide instead to pray for them. It's refreshing to know that each day you can start anew.

Here are some uplifting words from the esteemed Sadhguru, founder of the Isha Foundation in India: *"Do not try to fix whatever comes in your life. Fix yourself in such a way that whatever comes, you will be fine. You cannot suffer the past or future because they do not exist. What you are suffering is your memory and your imagination. Your thoughts and emotions are of no existential consequence. They are your creation—you could make them any way you want."*

It's difficult to argue with that. Indeed, our creations are entirely our own. Question your thoughts. Don't hold yourself hostage to a past that cannot be changed. Forgiving others and letting go—whether by tossing your burdens into the ocean or releasing them to the skies—can set you free. Someone must be the bigger person—let that someone be you. When you release, forgive, and forget, you demonstrate maturity and conserve valuable energy that would otherwise be wasted. Holding onto grudges or dwelling on small actions keeps us small and petty. As the saying goes, *nothing big ever came from being small!*

Although we can't change the past, you were ultimately the architect of your own decisions. Nobody else made those countless choices for you. Others may have influenced your decisions—you may have caved under pressure or even had someone take unfair advantage of you. But in the end, you invited them along for the ride, and you always had the power to stop the train. You may have seen red flags and chosen to remain silent, leading to an unmitigated disaster. Perhaps you failed to set or enforce boundaries, and things eventually went south.

Regardless, it's time to put it behind you. More often than not, you were at least 50 percent responsible for the outcome, and in many cases, you had the final say. See these experiences as lessons learned. Let go, take the high road, forgive, and embrace logic. I repeat: We can't change the past.

Moreover, consider taking responsibility for your own past actions. Is there someone you should apologize to—even if you believe they were petty or in the wrong? Imagine how much they would appreciate your thoughtfulness, how it might change their perception of you. From their perspective, it's not about who's right or wrong—it's about how they feel. By showing kindness, humility, and taking ownership of your actions, you position yourself as the bigger person. Apologizing isn't a sign of weakness; it's a testament to strength, confidence, and compassion.

Worry, stress, criticism, grudges, jealousy, fear, meanness, and lack of forgiveness are like pouring poison into your body—they damage your well-being. I am not a physician, but I have read many accounts of diseases and stress-related issues caused by intense mental struggles such as anxiety, anger, negativity, and depression. These mental states can manifest as physical pain and, in severe cases, can even lead to death. Negative self-talk and mental turmoil can push individuals into dire situations, deep depression, or physical illness.

Countless people have driven themselves to the brink through stress and negativity. When the human body endures extreme stress and anxiety, something inevitably must "give." The consequences can include ulcers, gastrointestinal issues, heart conditions, hypertension, obesity, and uncontrollable anger, often resulting in a sour and distasteful attitude toward life. Some individuals visibly exhibit their agony: bent over, stooped, gazing downward, oblivious to life's gorgeous possibilities. They fail to notice the stunning skies, inspiring opportunities, and beauty unfolding around them. Instead, they trap themselves in despair, creating a living hell through their own thought processes. For instance, one might say, "My father lost most of his funds in the stock market. God, I'm next." Pessimists often believe the world is ending without carefully analyzing the details or considering recovery options. Negative thought processes can turn into self-destructive prophecies, taking on a life of their own—becoming a living organism of despair and negativity entirely of their own making.

Conversely, there are those who have overcome disease through relentless determination and positive self-talk. Ambitious and positive individuals approach challenges with strategy and action rather than complaint. Movers and shakers turn challenges into opportunities. They understand that life is filled with ups and downs: economic fluctuations, bad luck, relationship difficulties, and unforeseen storms. They recognize that these storms strike unexpectedly—and they never stop coming. They remain prepared, focused on solutions, and resilient, knowing that most problems are fixable. They don't let their inner critics ruin their lives.

To be truly happy, it's important to let go of self-critical thoughts and simply BE. Refresh yourself—breathe deeply and do it now. Flow with whatever amazing thoughts come your way. When you're at peace with yourself, owning who you are becomes effortless.

You'll make thousands of decisions in your life, but what's done is done—whether it was a poor business decision or a wise choice to end a partnership. If things haven't worked out, it's time to move on. The sooner you learn from experiences and adapt along the way, the better your mindset and life will become. Happiness comes from putting the past behind you.

So don't second-guess yourself. You made the best decision you could at the time, based on the information and emotions you had. Forgive yourself and look back proudly on what you've learned. Celebrate your courage to put yourself out there and trying—because that's the primary benefit of every experience.

Motivational speaker, sports analyst, and legendary football coach Lou Holtz once said, "The biggest problem most people have is too good of a memory." This profound truth resonates in every aspect of life. Dwelling on past decisions, whether in your business or your personal life, often serves no purpose. Decisions can be based on facts, but they can also become overly emotional. It's easy to get sucked into a negative mindset, endlessly replaying what went wrong. What a grave waste of life's precious time and energy! Instead, learn, adapt, and move forward.

Embrace New Opportunities with a Positive Mindset

It's no surprise that the hardest workers appear to have unimpeded smooth sailing in life; but it's really the thousands of well-thought-out decisions, critical thinking, and thorough analyses that contribute to their success. It's their grit and relentless hard work.

The three C's: "Don't criticize, complain, or condemn"—are meaningful, concise words from famed author Dale Carnegie. Clear out the noise and focus. Don't get sidetracked by someone else's agenda, goals, priorities, or missions. If you get locked into a negative thought process, find soothing ways to clear it out. Listen to music, take a walk, help someone in need. It's good for the soul.

STREAMLINING OPERATIONS

SIMPLIFY YOUR LIFE BY ELIMINATING UNNECESSARY TASKS AND COMMITMENTS

Ensure your focus aligns with your desired career path and areas of interest; avoid wasting time on non-contributing activities. Look, listen, and observe. What do you do when you veer off course? Do you ignore red flags, choosing to ride it out instead? Do you sweep issues under the rug, creating a mess to deal with later—a "later" that often never comes?

You're not alone. It's easy to notice warning signs yet fail to adjust your course. Some even choose to see themselves as victims, asking, *who is to blame?* It's important to pause, observe, and take stock of where you stand. Implement corrective measures as soon as possible, especially in relationships. Address issues quickly, honestly, and directly to avoid feelings of helplessness or complacency.

If you're considering a potential partner, ask yourself: is this a relationship or an unfixable project? Could it be an impending disaster? Size up challenges right away. We set ourselves up for failure—or overwhelming consequences—when we deny the signs, neglect good advice, refuse to walk away when necessary, or fail to correct what could have been made right.

Are you using your head or your heart? Are you taking a practical approach or letting feelings guide every decision? Double-check your direction frequently and stay committed to your plan, realigning as needed. Others will respect your commitment, execution, and no-nonsense approach. Stay disciplined by setting up an efficient schedule with clear constraints and making sure there are no tasks on there that don't belong. Keep things simple. No time is wasted if you're steadily working toward a long-term goal. Focus on the task at hand, enjoy the process of growth, and stick to your schedule.

Finally, trust your instincts. Listen to that soft whisper in the back of your mind—it's there to guide you. If you feel a sense of alignment and clarity, you're on the right course.

Align Your Priorities with Your Core Values

Brutal honesty with yourself is the foundation for launching anything meaningful, whether in financial pursuits, personal growth, long-term planning, or education. This kind of fulfillment feels deeply right—empowering and resonating with the effort you've invested. It is drawn from your experiences and the wisdom of your genuine thoughts and beliefs, and it's guided by your values, ethics, and most importantly, your soul—not the expectations of friends or colleagues.

You don't want to look back on your life and realize you lived as a pleaser, shaping your journey around others' dreams, definitions of success, or expectations while neglecting your own. Let your decisions flow from the heart and soul.

Ultimately, it's your ideas and strategic approach that will create a sense of fulfillment. Surround yourself with pictures of progress or loved ones at your desk—things that evoke feelings of love and achievement—your life purpose. These reminders mirror who you are as you work, what you've achieved, and mostly, why you're here. Notice how little adjustments like this make you feel ... tweaking and tailoring as you go.

Genuine creation—born purely from your own thoughts and inspirations, untouched by external influences—is one of life's most rewarding and visceral experiences. I begin with nothing but a blank sheet of paper before sketching a home design or writing a song.

Consider this: some compliments you've received may have been for things that held little personal significance to you—perhaps fleeting trends or achievements that came at a low or vulnerable moment. Seeking validation for pursuits that don't align with your true values can lead to a hollow existence.

So make sure your choices truly resonate with you. When you align with your authentic self, it's as natural as breathing—an effortless groove. From there, you can ride the wave of your true mission and defined purpose, experiencing a life of profound meaning and joy.

AVOIDING UNSATISFACTORY PARTNERSHIPS

Evaluate Potential Collaborators by Starting Small

Learn to recognize the value different people bring. Rookies can offer fresh energy and enthusiasm, while seasoned veterans provide wisdom and a broader perspective. Approach relationships with the mindset of "trust but verify." While paranoia is counterproductive, exercising prudent judgment is essential. Request references, gather multiple bids, and seek expert opinions before making significant decisions.

Take charge and remain vigilant. Conduct trial runs before advancing to higher levels of engagement, especially with tasks requiring trust. If hiring someone for your home, start with small projects to assess their abilities. Trial runs reveal much—communication skills, timeliness, accountability, billing accuracy, craftsmanship, professionalism, and reliability in meeting deadlines. This due diligence is especially crucial in sensitive areas like childcare or other responsibilities where negligence can have dire consequences.

Disappointments are inevitable; that's just part of life. Adopt a realistic outlook. Facing the truth—no matter how inconvenient—helps mitigate the risks of poor planning, which can otherwise lead to setbacks in both your career and personal life.

The most severe consequences often stem from deceiving ourselves, failing to see things with clarity and balance. A realistic perspective keeps your efforts aligned with reality. Avoid obscuring the authentic truth of the people or situations around you. Failing to acknowledge reality fosters dismay and creates an ongoing feeling of incongruence.

END RELATIONSHIPS AND PARTNERSHIPS THAT DRAIN YOUR ENERGY

Life's journey inevitably includes some regrettable pit stops—encounters with false friends and big talkers who rarely deliver on their promises. If you find yourself in the wrong place with the wrong people, exit gracefully. You'll be grateful you did.

Have you ever met someone who still complains about another person's actions years later—only to embody the very traits they once despised? It's as if they're unknowingly replicating the same behavior they abhorred, treating others in the exact way they once condemned. For example, they might say, *"My mother always talked about herself, and it drove me crazy. She was such a narcissist."* Yet, moments later, they launch into a long-winded monologue about their own struggles, talking over you, speaking *at* you rather than *to* you, and failing to engage in a real conversation. It's almost laughable.

I've witnessed this dynamic more than once. After exhausting themselves with their one-sided diatribe, they'll eventually pause and ask, *"So what have you been up to?"* Often, I respond with silence—then ask a question to redirect the conversation, testing whether they're actually done. Their lack of self-awareness can be astonishing. They don't see the irony of their actions, and maybe, they simply aren't wired to.

Remember, a conversation should go two ways. Do you put yourself in the other person's shoes when you talk to them? When meeting someone for the first time, you cannot know what they've been through in life. Yet, it's common to rush to judgment based on their appearance, education, car, or profession. What we fail to consider are the unseen battles they may be fighting—whether mental, emotional, or in their private lives. Often, the most profound struggles lie in the unseen and unspoken. Life can thrust immeasurable challenges upon people, many of which are far beyond their control.

Cultivating compassion will always benefit you in this life. If someone seems worn down by the weight of their day—or by life itself—take a moment to check in with them. Even if you don't know them well, a kind gesture can go a long way. Ask if they're all right, inject a touch of humor, or find another way to brighten their day.

For some, the toll of life may have been too great, leaving them embittered or sorrowful and beyond the reach of outside help. Nothing you say or do may alter their course. This can serve as a reminder to avoid letting life's struggles suck the life out of us entirely. Perspective is key. When we know someone's full story, their bitterness or sadness often becomes more understandable. But don't overthink it—it's easy to drive yourself crazy trying to piece it all together.

Be wary also of overly optimistic dreamers who talk a big game but struggle to take meaningful action. When confronted with dishonesty, distance yourself immediately. You'll be happier when you let go of the past and stop second-guessing yourself. If a relationship with someone is draining your energy, end it.

You made the best decisions you could at the time, based on the information you had and the feelings you experienced. Over the years, you've become wiser, learning where to invest your time and who contributes to your success.

Seek Out Positive and Supportive Connections

Surround yourself with people who uplift and support you, creating a life filled with optimism and positivity. We become like the people we surround ourselves with. Misery loves company, so let those individuals congregate—but don't fall into their trap. Instead, lead by example: be a doer. Taking action energizes you. When you put in the work and follow through to 100 percent completion, the process itself becomes empowering.

Spend your time with goal-oriented, like-minded individuals who inspire and elevate you. A positive mindset is their greatest asset—a million-dollar gift that costs absolutely nothing.

Have you noticed that most of the things you worry about never actually happen? Reflect on the major challenges you've faced. You're still here—you survived them all. Life is full of decisions, big and small, and it's how we choose to react that defines us. Those with a positive mindset quickly accept and resolve setbacks, relentlessly moving forward with confidence and contagious energy.

When you cultivate positive thoughts, your belief systems radiate uplifting energy. Take time to look through old pictures of loved ones you cherish or memorable trips you've taken. This simple act is incredibly effective—it fuels you forward, reminding you of your potential, your joy, and the essence of who you are. Show your appreciation to the people who've been part of your journey by expressing gratitude—they have helped shape who you are today. Unfortunately, many miss this critical step.

When you encounter friends or family trapped in a negative thought process, gravitate instead toward those who exude enthusiasm, happiness, and positive energy. It's about finding what works for you—your comfort zone and happy place—combined with what makes you feel your best.

Surround yourself with colleagues you truly enjoy working with, individuals who share your career-based love language—that is, the ways people feel appreciated and valued at work. Some want praise, others prefer tangible gifts, help, or mentorship. The internet expands your possibilities—seek out common interests, groups, vendors, and start-ups. The end goal is to find and engage with *your* people.

10
NAVIGATE FAMILY AND SOCIAL PRESSURES

Family and societal expectations can be challenging. Stay true to yourself and pursue a life that aligns with your values and passions.

THIS CHAPTER COVERS:

Dealing with Opinions of Family Members
- *Respectfully consider family opinions but stay true to your own values.*
- *Communicate your goals and aspirations clearly.*

Blazing Your Own Trail
- *Follow your own path and pursue what makes you happy.*
- *Do not let others dictate your life's direction.*

DEALING WITH OPINIONS OF FAMILY MEMBERS

Respectfully Consider Family Opinions but Stay True to Your Own Values

Do you find yourself worrying about what family members think of you? Why give it so much power? Worrying won't change anything—it only wastes time and energy. This is your life, and you deserve to be happy. Prioritizing yourself doesn't mean being selfish, narcissistic, or egotistical. Pursue your goals for the right reasons—with joy, humility, and a heart for others. True fulfillment comes when we step outside ourselves and serve. Whether it's faith, family, or giving back to the community that brings you meaning, go after it with purpose. Make an impact.

Taking advice from friends and family can be likened to seeking legal counsel from a non-lawyer friend. This cycle continues because sharing our fears and doubts with a friend often validates our concerns; misery loves company. But a family member's opinion is just that—a thought or opinion, nothing more. They're simply giving you a piece of their mind.

As for intentionally irritating comments from family, a friend once said, "They know which buttons to push because they installed them." If you're unfortunate enough to have such a character in your life, take the high road. Ignoring them may work. Resist wrestling with the pig in the mud.

Family pressure or expectations may be tied to occupation histories, private schooling, and funding—and in these core matters, disagreements can often intensify. Rebelling at a young age is normal. It can escalate in the teenage years, becoming more intense. Disagreements can arise over educational expenses, coursework a parent may not believe in, or lack of support.

Stay focused and aggressively pursue your dreams. You'll be amazed at how many lives you'll touch through a craft you love.

Even taking the time to share the truth about hardships or the success stories you or your family has experienced could spark a breakthrough. This openness might even encourage others to share their own stories.

COMMUNICATE YOUR GOALS AND ASPIRATIONS CLEARLY

When you speak to family members about your life, communicate clearly and without an agenda. If they don't like what you're doing, that's okay. They don't have to like it. We can hope they'll be supportive, but we are not responsible for their feelings.

Family members must respect boundaries. If a full disagreement arises, have an honest conversation. If it's a control issue, where they demand you follow their plan, suggest speaking with a therapist; either of these could be an effective first step. In any case, family can be the most challenging when it comes to dictating the options for a proposed direction. Those with intense reactions may benefit from anger management counsel. You might also suggest a hobby that makes them happy, helping to divert their attention elsewhere.

Here's an example of family decision-making: you feel that all the responsibility of caring for aging parents rests entirely on your shoulders. Speak up to your siblings. Be honest, get it off your chest. Get the conversation started or watch it worsen. Your siblings cannot read your mind, nor have they witnessed your efforts behind the scenes. Be proactive. You don't know what meltdown may await down the road, where everyone is at odds. Never be rude or bitter but speak up or it will worsen.

By doing your part—communicating your concerns and creating a game plan—you've done your best. Instead of issuing demands or imposing expectations, ask family members questions. Recognize that their perspectives matter as much as yours. Refrain from giving orders like a drill sergeant or barking commands. Be aware that many people become defensive even when you are simply addressing mutual concerns or asking direct questions. Anything condescending, one-sided, or poorly thought-out is likely to come back and bite you.

It's fascinating how the power of the spoken word can be received—impactful, misinterpreted, or even duplicitous, depending on intent, emotion, and body language. If you're an athlete and your father repeatedly says he was never good at sports, but he hopes things work out, you may feel unsupported. Hearing these statements daily can be demoralizing and may give the impression that his worldview is dictated solely by his own experiences. Don't take it personally. Stick with whatever is positive and focus on spreading love and kindness.

BLAZING YOUR OWN TRAIL

Follow Your Own Path and Pursue What Makes You Happy

Family members may try to dictate who or what you should be. Don't let this happen. Blaze your own trail, block out the noise, and follow your gut and inner guidance. While we may respect and admire the achievements of our family members, whether successful or not, we should never compare ourselves to them. Instead, let yourself be guided by your heartfelt beliefs and pursue endeavors that resonate with you. Share your unique skills, talents, and gifts with the world, and define the true you.

Self-discovery requires peeling back layers of superficiality and leads to increased self-awareness and genuine happiness. This is where true transformation occurs—reflected in your eyes, radiating confidence and embodying your life's purpose.

Challenge conventional thinking and old conditioning by brainstorming ideas that go against your family's norms, reflecting on what truly brings you joy. Embrace new experiences and challenges, and don't fear disappointment or failure. Successful people aren't fundamentally different from you; they simply put their abilities into action. What others do, say, or think about you is none of your business. Opinions, short-sightedness, misunderstandings, perspectives, and goals vary for everyone. We are all unique, like juxtaposed test tubes in a lab, each differentiated by our own distinct formula.

Ultimately, when you take charge, you'll realize that only *you* could've tailored things to your unique preferences and navigated a path that's enjoyable for you. Things are only 'done right' when you call the shots, engineering routes with a clear, point-to-point plan, well thought out. Mind your business, stay focused, and remain disciplined every step of the way—things work out.

DO NOT LET OTHERS DICTATE YOUR LIFE'S DIRECTION

Be intentional about the company you keep. Negative influences can drain your energy and poison your mindset. Optimists thrive on hope, hard work, and possibility, whereas defeatists spiral into frustration and stagnation. Eliminate sources of negativity and focus on nurturing relationships and habits that propel you forward. Your time is one of your most precious resources; guard it fiercely and spend it wisely.

Don't limit or compare yourself. Your family's or others' ideas will never define you. Without effort, nothing changes. "Bold moves or nothing happens," as Rolling Stones rocker Keith Richards put it. His words challenge mediocrity. Taking no action, you have no one to blame but yourself. Think back—weren't the bold moves you tackled head-on the very things that fixed or significantly improved your situation? Progress comes from action, not hesitation. Following your instincts and your inner compass is crucial; imitating others will not bring true fulfillment.

Shine as the happiest person in the room with the biggest smile. Stay grounded, humble, compassionate, and steadfast in your unique journey, guided by carefully selected choices. In this dance of life, adjust as you go, tailoring your decisions to meet your current needs. Everything changes; nothing stays the same—new players will enter your orbit. Economic vicissitudes may throw you off course or even worse. A shift in short-term or long-term goals will emerge. Be decisive, reevaluate, and reset your game plan.

11
NETWORK AND LEARN

Building a network of supportive and knowledgeable individuals will greatly enhance your personal and professional growth. Learn from industry leaders and use networking as a tool for advancement.

THIS CHAPTER COVERS:

Networking Strategies
- *Get to know all kinds of people.*
- *Build genuine connections and offer value to others.*

Learning from Industry Leaders
- *Seek mentorship and advice from experienced professionals.*
- *Continually educate yourself and stay updated in your field.*

NETWORKING STRATEGIES

GET TO KNOW ALL KINDS OF PEOPLE

Each progressive step you take is huge—whether forging new friendships, joining clubs, engaging in athletics, or starting a men's or women's group—broadens your horizons and represents an investment in yourself—reflecting your varied interests and self-expression.

Get to know people who may not share your inclinations. Everyone is different. Some are "thinkers," responding primarily from an intellectual standpoint, while others are "feelers," driven by emotion and sensitivity. Then there are slow, methodical movers who blend emotion with pragmatism, carefully weighing options before acting. Bridging these gaps is key—whether you're engaging with a fast-paced city dweller or a rural farmer.

Consider your audience—their eye contact, demeanor, priorities, expertise, and ability to synthesize information. Take the time to connect with those outside your usual circles and discover what makes them tick. Be honest about your goals, intentions, and the spirit behind your work. Learn about their priorities, timelines, and energy levels.

As you get acquainted, you gain valuable insights and sharpen your own focus. You may also identify areas that need strengthening to align with your aspirations—even within rigid bureaucratic systems. The more perspectives you engage with, the more light you cast onto unseen challenges, finding common ground even with those whose nature seems opposite to your own.

Difficult encounters often teach us more than the great days. Stumbles, falls, and failures serve as valuable lessons. We take note, make corrections, and avoid repeating mistakes by resetting our game plan. Real learning happens here, not when everything is perfect. Laugh, and don't take things too seriously—present your authentic self and *keep it real*.

Networking cross-functionally can also lead to finding common ground for future collaborations. Loosen your grip and make a 180-degree decision, trying out an entirely new career from a fun hobby or side hustle. Focus on what you can take away from each experience, connecting the dots and embracing your sweet spot; set incremental goals to build on the experiences you love most.

When it comes to networking, stop in at your favorite coffee spots, the library, or a community center for a break. A librarian's book idea could change your life! Preemptively scan local event magazines to stay ahead of upcoming happenings; don't wait until the last minute on things. Attend work sessions—eclectic souls abound there, including old friends and new leads. Even club ideas can be sparked for *you* to take the lead. Quick stopovers may lead to something new and, over time, can present huge growth opportunities. Work your way from the top down.

Do something different every day. Quick segues can surprise you in a good way. When out and about, pay attention to ad boards and local publications—they may spark new ideas. Follow up on leads and be assertive. Be a voracious reader of periodicals, research your options—LEAN in. That's when ideas turn into your fireworks! You're unstoppable when you manifest, feel, learn, then grow.

Build Genuine Connections and Offer Value to Others

Winning the day means striving to be the best version of yourself while putting others first. Morals, ethics, character, integrity and team work will guide you through every challenge. When you prioritize people and community over personal gain and material possessions, you create a foundation for true fulfillment. Fearless, courageous, open-minded, kind—you stand out.

If you feel isolated or lonely, make it a habit to reach out to two or three people each week with sincere, positive compassion and uplifting messages. Inquire about details in an authentic way, greeting them with positivity. This sets a tone of boundless energy and love that radiates from the heart. Consider the many lives you'll touch through your personal contributions—both by finding your people and supporting them. Good feelings will always best monetary elements.

Keep things professional: if you have nothing nice to say, say nothing. Unfortunately, many people struggle to say something kind to or about others. It speaks volumes about their character if they cannot recognize the talents of those around them. This could be due to feelings of competition, jealousy, insecurity, or misery—perhaps fearing they'll lose the race of life by lifting others up or speaking highly of them. It's okay for everyone to win and be happy.

If you struggle to compliment others, reflect on what might be holding you back. Are you easily envious, even when others have put in the hard work? Be the bigger person. Encouraging others spreads kindness selflessly and peacefully. Observe the amazing kindness they return to you!

Share all your talents, push your limits, and embody an intensity fueled by your gifts and abilities. Inspire others along the way. You never know who you may have inspired yesterday. Perhaps there's an art or skill within you waiting for expression, now evoked and released. As was once said, "Cemeteries are full of people with songs in them." This means that many who've passed had vast, untapped abilities they never expressed or shared. Don't let that be you. Share yourself and show us who you truly are.

Whether it's fear of failure, embarrassment, lack of confidence, or a lack of encouragement, a lot gets left on the table—actually, left in the cemetery. Practicing leadership fosters learning, striving, expanding your reach, enhancing communication skills, and unlocking potential. Leadership builds confidence, whereas following instructions can be a slower path. Taking full responsibility is exhilarating.

Building a team around big ideas and targeted goals you've been considering can start with gathering a few trusted friends to bounce ideas off. As new sparks light up, pursue the idea further by meeting with consultants or experts. Is there a point where things start to look promising, or are they heading south? Watch for red flags or that feeling of a fledgling idea sinking.

However, be cautious not to give away your hard-earned ideas, as others may potentially steal them. "Keep your business to yourself" remains a trusted line of demarcation to maintain. Consider discussing similar ideas, but not the exact ones, testing them out by passing them by experts. This way, your specific strategies and course of action are kept safe from being copied. Consulting with a patent attorney might be necessary, depending on how solidified your concept and game plan are. There are entrepreneurial competition TV shows with elimination processes and strategies that could hone your moves.

The more ideas you have and pursue, the better. Multiple concepts and strategic moves you're considering can manifest and become a force in motion.

Avoid defeatists. Hire remarkable professionals who are results-driven, considered the best of the best. If partnering with others isn't imperative, pursue your goals independently—it's your decision. Always be kind and professional. Walk away if something feels incongruent, even if you can't explain it. Later, the reason will likely come full circle, confirming your initial gut instincts.

LEARNING FROM INDUSTRY LEADERS

Seek Mentorship and Advice from Experienced Professionals

Build a network that encourages and inspires you. Along the pathway to self-discovery, self-improvement, and self-love, there's comfort in a team or extended family—friends and consultants to lean on for technical advice across various disciplines. Some hire a coach or personal trainer, but self-motivation, research, and putting yourself out there socially can save you a lot of time and money. The more you take on yourself, the more your strength and confidence will build and radiate. At the same time, you don't need to wear every hat. Know your "go-to" professionals for each element. Talk to three experts before making big decisions.

When reaching out to industry leaders and building a network, start at the top and work your way down—it's a highly effective strategy. Connecting with industry leaders and professionals opens you to a wealth of knowledge and new opportunities. Engage with experts to gain invaluable insights from the best in the field, whether it's from a top-tier accounting firm, a renowned library, an esteemed medical facility, a thriving design firm, or a leading hedge fund. Top firms earn their reputation through excellence and through upholding proven and ethical practices.

Tony Bennett's impact on basketball extends far beyond the game. As head coach at the University of Virginia, he shaped not just skilled players but exceptional people. When he announced his retirement during the writing of this book, it marked the end of an extraordinary era. His players describe him not only as a brilliant coach but, more importantly, as an even better human being. Even after winning a national championship, humility remained his defining trait. Imagine achieving such success while being known most for your character—a rarity in today's world.

I once had the privilege of meeting Tony Bennett in a parking lot, and even in that brief moment, his genuine smile and character shone through. One can't help but wonder about the values instilled in him—ethics, leadership, faith, and compassion—that shaped such an extraordinary individual. If you entrusted him with your most valuable possessions, there's no doubt he'd handle them with absolute integrity, even without knowing you. A world full of people like Bennett might not need locks, police, or courtrooms. He embodies what we aspire to in our children, communities, and ourselves. In moments of doubt, I often ask, *"What would Tony do?"* His integrity is a rare yet timeless model for ethical living. Imagine if more leaders followed his example. People like him are unforgettable—true class acts.

When you find yourself among a new group of people excelling in character or craft, it's essential to remember that we're all created equal. Stay calm, confident, and composed—there's no need to feel intimidated. Your time will come. Avoid rushing in with assumptions or quick judgments. Instead, maintain control of your thoughts and reactions, understanding that your primary responsibility is to direct your mind and respond with grace. Stay focused on your goals and what you hope to gain from the experience.

Approaching new situations with an open mind creates space for deeply rewarding growth. By staying in your lane, honing your listening skills, and fostering thoughtful communication, you'll be appreciated as someone who genuinely engages with others. This poise and presence often lead to being welcomed back into valuable circles, further enriching your journey.

Observe everything around you and assess if you still align with the puzzle you originally envisioned for yourself. Life's twists and turns may prompt you to pivot or adjust, and that's perfectly natural. You owe it to the world to share your unique talents, skills, and inspiration, spreading love and positivity through your contributions. Remember, we are often our own harshest critics.

Continually Educate Yourself and Stay Updated in Your Field

Investing in yourself allows you to become multitalented and seasoned over time. Being over-prepared and ready for game time is what others expect from a professional. For me, this journey began with training in engineering at a young age. It progressed to project management, construction, and eventually music performance, recording thirteen albums in thirteen years. This path demanded problem-solving, number crunching, understanding economics, honing organizational skills, assembling winning teams, and carefully selecting talent. Excuses were never an option—completing every task and preparing for worst-case scenarios with backup plans always in place was a non-negotiable standard.

Once developed, these skills proved to be versatile and cross-functional, adaptable to countless other challenges and situations in the years and storms ahead. It's highly advantageous to possess multiple skills and be prepared for action. You will encounter a wide variety of personalities, each with their own expectations, goals, rules, egos, quirks, and inevitable delays.

Multitalented entrepreneurs wear many hats as they navigate economic fluctuations, regulations, requirements, inflation, architectural review committees, and financing. However, there are only so many hours in a day. A builder may choose to contract out aspects of the project and might oversee twenty subcontractors, making it easy to see *system overload* rearing its head.

Read books relevant to your craft or curiosity, engage in soul-searching, and focus on honing specific skills—each one a piece of the puzzle. Setting goals and holding yourself accountable should be central to your plan. Never stop learning or reading and explore the history of your craft to understand the challenges others have overcome. An avalanche of success could be just around the corner, but it requires tactical, well-researched moves. Prioritize your goals, follow a plan, and test out ideas. Take safe, calculated steps!

The more you accomplish on your own, the more confident you become. Through self-reflection and brutal honesty, you begin to drill deeply into your purpose. It's crucial to address potential hang-ups upfront, preempting any issues that could derail your plans. Whether you're seeking legal or financial advice or making any other serious decision, think carefully. Deeply consider your options before taking *any* action. While this advice may seem trite, its value is immense. Details reveal everything, so proceed with caution.

No question is a dumb question. Always confirm with basic, open-ended inquiries—it's surprising how often you and others may not be on the same page. Avoid rushing; ensure all agreements are signed by both parties before proceeding. Negotiate, edit, fix, restart, and rethink worst-case scenarios. Take time to mull over your plan—say, five to ten days, meticulously reviewing its status and assessing how various factors may be influencing each other. Connect the dots and retrace the steps that brought you to this point. Ask yourself: am I on track to achieve my end goal? What do I truly want out of this experience? Am I collaborating with the best partners or simply settling? Do I take advice and genuinely listen to constructive criticism or is my ego getting in the way? What is best for my community? Are my motives altruistic or self-serving? Do I feel balanced, or do I have a plan to get there?

The best entrepreneurs I've encountered approach life this way—asking direct, critical questions. They fortify their plans and keep moving forward, consulting experts, running numbers, seeking new ideas and investments, reading challenging books, and constantly brainstorming their next best moves.

Their success comes from a rhythm of continuous forward motion powered by determination. They stay alert, recognizing pitfalls, fees, and hidden soft costs. They catch every detail, cautiously verifying all aspects while questioning others and reviewing annual returns. Methodically and efficiently, they work through the gears of progress, clicking through options with diligence and focus.

Rebounding and multitasking—amidst the diverse subjects you engage with—are powerful forms of self-investment. By striving for growth, you become stronger, more balanced, articulate, and educated. With the right mindset, forward motion creates equilibrium, allowing you to prosper and thrive across all aspects of life. Investing in yourself brings a sense of empowerment, generating remarkable energy and competence.

Your best self, operating at the highest level, pushes boundaries you once feared. More importantly, your skill set and self-confidence prepare you for unforeseen challenges—recessions, depressions, or even a failed business. Investing in yourself strengthens your assets and hones your ability to pivot on a dime when unexpected changes throw you off course. Like a fearless, well-trained athlete, you reset your offense, calculate risks, analyze finances, and put a new plan in place before launching again. Listen closely to your advisors and question the details as if you know their job as well as they do. If you find you know it better, it's probably time to replace them.

These changes, accompanied by growing confidence, transform you into a modern-day Renaissance soul—a vibrant, more colorful version of yourself, equipped with the resources, self-esteem, and determination to ignite any mission. It's not just about monetary gain or potential—it's about the feeling of renewal, progress, and possibility. The journey itself becomes its own reward.

12
DEVELOP RESILIENCE

Resilience is key to handling setbacks and challenges. Embrace difficulties as opportunities for growth and keep moving forward.

THIS CHAPTER COVERS:

Handling Setbacks
- View setbacks as learning experiences.
- Consider key financial building blocks.
- Develop a plan to overcome obstacles and bounce back stronger.

Developing Resilience
- Cultivate a mindset of perseverance and determination.
- Stay focused on your long-term goals despite short-term challenges.

HANDLING SETBACKS

VIEW SETBACKS AS LEARNING EXPERIENCES

Setbacks are an inevitable part of life, shaping and strengthening you. The key lies in working through them, letting go of past mistakes, and channeling your energy into "fix mode." Developing the skill to be a fixer—someone who can tackle challenges and find solutions—is invaluable. It's not just a skill; it's a mindset that equips you with resilience and adaptability, attributes you'll cherish throughout life. As the saying goes, "There are no dress rehearsals in life." This reminder emphasizes the importance of living fully, tackling problems head-on, and embracing the real moments.

Problem-solving can even be enjoyable—an exercise in creativity and perseverance. When you look back, those moments of struggle often become your greatest teachers, sparking growth and revealing strength you didn't know you had. Confidence is built not by avoiding storms, but by facing and withstanding their unpredictable ferocity. Sit complacently, and growth will stagnate.

In some ways, life mirrors the stock market, with its steady upward trends during bull markets and sudden storms of bear market corrections that test your resilience. Success is found in how you navigate those downturns, coming out stronger and wiser each time.

CONSIDER KEY FINANCIAL BUILDING BLOCKS

After recovering from a setback, you must create a robust plan for your financial future. Begin by laying down a strong foundation of assets on something as simple as a spreadsheet. Use this as your "dream sheet"—a fun exercise to set ambitious goals and trace them backward to actionable steps. Imagine yourself ten years from now and create a detailed vision of financial freedom. Go big; don't limit your aspirations.

- Here are some vehicles to consider: Retirement accounts: Calculate contributions to a Roth IRA or 401(k). Even small, consistent investments, like $100 per week, grow exponentially over time thanks to compound interest.

- Rental properties: Research the costs, potential returns, and financing options. This could be a solid addition to your wealth portfolio.

- Stock market investments: Start with small blue-chip stock positions. These stocks are reliable performers that can weather market fluctuations.

- Healthcare and benefits: Maximize any employer-provided benefits packages, including matching retirement contributions, insurance, and tax-advantaged savings accounts (like HSAs).

Once you've identified your goals, plug in starting points for deposits. Begin exploring financing options if real estate is part of your vision. Consulting a trusted, certified financial advisor can transform this plan into actionable strategies with professional guidance tailored to your goals and risk tolerance.

Yes, the process might feel mundane or tedious—investing and financial planning are more like planting a tree than chasing fireworks. Yet over thirty-plus years, the small seeds you plant today can multiply into an abundant forest. Your future self will thank you, celebrating with cartwheels or backflips, all thanks to the patience and pragmatism you exercise today. Remember, "a failure to plan is a plan for failure." Take it step by step and the results will amaze you.

Outside of finances, invest your time deliberately in activities that not only challenge you but also bring joy and personal growth. Life is unpredictable and tomorrow isn't guaranteed—so focus on experiences that enrich your journey. The value of memories, relationships, and achievements far outweighs material gains in the long run. Prioritizing this over instant gratification ensures a deeper and more rewarding path.

The pursuit of lasting success demands discipline and commitment. Progress comes from consistent effort and follow-through, not from shortcuts or fleeting moments of satisfaction. Success stories are written by those who embrace accountability, confront challenges, and understand the "why" behind their actions. Conversely, defeatist attitudes thrive on excuses and external blame—reasons for failure that distance them from meaningful progress.

Develop a Plan to Overcome Obstacles and Bounce Back Stronger

After rebounding from what feels like a setback, recognize it for what it is—an experience or a thought, not an insurmountable failure. Often, your competitive nature or self-critical mindset creates a narrative that hinders progress. Let go of perfectionism and overthinking; instead, focus on being present while making steady, incremental advances. Remember the wisdom of "The turtle always beats the hare"—success built on slow, steady, honest efforts endures.

Consider this analogy: a builder with eighty homes under construction simultaneously may end up with the same net assets in two decades as someone who carefully builds one home at a time with precision and focus. Why? When endeavors grow too large too quickly, the risk increases exponentially. One supply chain disruption, market downturn, or economic crisis can trigger a domino effect of chaos, stress, and financial strain.

Avoid the trap of ego-driven ambitions or the need to prove your worth through relentless growth. Chasing aggressive milestones for the sake of status or validation can backfire in an instant—a week of bad news is all it takes to bring an entire empire crumbling down. Stay grounded in your purpose. Build with care, patience, and sustainability. True success doesn't require flashy displays of power or capitalistic excess. It thrives in consistency, resilience, and the peace of knowing your foundation is solid—even in the face of unexpected challenges.

When rebounding in life, it's invaluable to set a long-term vision while creating manageable short-term goals—monthly, bimonthly, or six-month progress charts. Write these goals down, track them closely, and rework the numbers to ensure realistic outcomes. Regularly assess your progress, financial gains or losses, and other significant benchmarks. Use this feedback loop to recalibrate your approach. Beyond that, longer-term goals of one to three years can give you a broader horizon to work toward and a greater sense of purpose. Having something tangible to look forward to fuels excitement and optimism about the future.

It's equally essential to develop an exit strategy when progress stalls. Whether you're rethinking a career, a project, or personal growth, no one will chart your course for you. Take charge, face challenges head-on, and work through problems one by one. Time is finite, so know when to cut your losses and shift gears. Celebrate small wins and milestones, acknowledging every step forward while preparing for new endeavors.

Some of humanity's most beautiful creations—songs, business breakthroughs, books that stir the soul—often arise in the aftermath of storms. Difficult moments have a way of focusing our thoughts, pushing us to new creative heights and helping us tap into depths we might not access in times of ease. Even at your lowest, don't lose faith. Instead, lean into that storm—greatness often emerges there. When the dust settles, you'll look back and realize those challenges paved the way for your most inspired and transformative work.

Avoiding "I" is critical when making decisions, particularly during times of uncertainty. Overthinking can bog you down, and constantly questioning your next move can stall progress. Have an expert by your side for each challenge instead of playing hero or wearing ten different specialist hats.

It's essential to know when to act decisively and when to step back and wait for the right opportunity. Patience is a powerful tool—the key is waiting for the best moment rather than forcing things to fit. Think of it like a surfer slowly paddling, allowing time for the right wave to come. In the same way, you need to wait for the right entry point, whether you're healing or preparing for a new venture. Once you've caught that wave, enjoy it fully and don't try to manipulate the moment. Don't overthink, overcompensate, or feel undeserving of success. Instead, lean into your confidence, cultivate your craft, and inspire others with your authenticity. BUT: In life, *don't let perfect become the enemy of good.* Perfect may never arrive. Lowering expectations is your best friend; anything extra is gravy, so to speak.

When the time is right, give it everything you've got. Don't be afraid to crush it—and then do it again, as long as your momentum carries you forward. It's all about understanding timing and being ready to seize the right opportunities when they align with your vision and dedication.

In every interview with highly respected souls such as Oprah Winfrey, Warren Buffett or Tony Robbins, they shared the same answer when asked what they did most: **READING** hundreds of books. Reading and acting on what they learned was essential to their success. Follow your curiosities and head to the library: INVEST IN YOURSELF!

DEVELOPING RESILIENCE

Cultivate a Mindset of Perseverance and Determination

Life truly is a continual process of resetting and refining your approach. It's about starting new ventures, evaluating what's working, feeling out the right team members, and doing more of what leads to smooth progress and fewer obstacles.

As you work through this, it's key to remember the importance of balance—make decisions logically and pragmatically, without being overly swayed by emotions. Aligning your goals with practical aspects of your life—your economic conditions, your environment, and your gut instincts—forms the solid foundation for sustainable progress. Taking breaks between major decisions is critical. Allow yourself the space to step back, breathe, and process without rushing. Making decisions from a calm, grounded place helps you avoid impulsive or poorly thought-out choices.

Life, by nature, involves constant trial and error. It's all about identifying weaknesses, analyzing them, and making adjustments that keep your long-term objectives in focus. Ultimately, everything is a process. With each step, you're evolving, learning, and recalibrating in ways that align with both your immediate needs and your overarching goals. Embrace the ebb and flow of this cycle and recognize that each setback or challenge offers another valuable lesson on the road to progress. Multitask: having many wheels turning gives you many options!

Virginia Secretary of Labor G. Bryan Slater's journey is a testament to resilience and determination. Raised in a financially struggling family, he faced immense challenges from the start. Yet, instead of yielding, he turned adversity into fuel for his drive. Nothing was handed to him. He worked his way through college at K-Mart, enduring harsh conditions—including sleeping in a closet with only an extension cord for power. Without parental guidance, encouragement, or a safety net, he relied solely on grit and tenacity to propel himself forward.

Slater embodies the spirit of the American dream, proving that perseverance and self-belief can overcome even the toughest odds. His ascent, holding positions as both Secretary of Administration and later, Secretary of Labor, reflects a career built on relentless focus and skill refinement. Each obstacle strengthened his resolve, making him a confident and multifaceted leader. The *10,000-hour rule* speaks to mastery through dedication—Slater exemplifies this principle. His relentless commitment to growth and improvement defied the odds, leading to remarkable success. With an unshakable "never-quit" attitude, he pursued his vision while lifting others along the way.

Your own utopian lifestyle or Garden of Eden won't be realized unless you do the work. Sketch out a game plan, get moving, set aside your fears and anxieties, and start acting toward your goals. Kick some ass, bypassing naysayers or anyone holding you back. This is your life.

Even the best of the best has been hit with huge setbacks. Many have suffered tragic ones. So many things may seem unfair, or truly are—skiers crash, filmmakers can't launch projects despite borrowing untold thousands, entire auto departments in Detroit are laid off, positions in corporations are eliminated. Family members disappoint, set you up for failure, and turn out to be characters you need to distance yourself from, if not completely silence.

The list of potential speed bumps is endless, unfortunately, but never feel discouraged or alone. You will emerge stronger through life's vicissitudes. They make you tough and resilient in situations where perseverance and grit remain paramount.

Try maintaining the mindset that something truly great is just around the corner. If you keep pushing and trying out new ideas, something will eventually break through that you can build upon. Good things happen to good people. And that means you!

Stay Focused on Your Long-Term Goals Despite Short-Term Challenges

When you're back to feeling like yourself after any rebounds or setbacks, you'll experience an empowering feeling within you that's hard to put into words—like reconnecting with the old you. It's a release of powerful endorphins that fuel forward momentum and better decision-making. It's a comfortable, strong, and confident feeling, like being part of a great team, all in balance. It's like a pottery wheel spinning smoothly at 300 RPMs—no vibration, just a soft, steady hum. That's when you've reached alignment and balance, much like the satisfying feeling exercise gives you.

You achieved it by simply being yourself, staying true to your beliefs, and letting life unfold naturally. Along the way, you supported others, despite facing more setbacks, disappointments, and tragedies than you could have ever counted.

And that is what we call *L-I-F-E.*

It's funny—at twenty, we feel invincible, certain we have all the answers. Yet by sixty, life's endless surprises and storms can leave us feeling like we know nothing at all.

The actress Hilary Swank, who grew up in a trailer park and even slept in her car in Los Angeles, stayed true to her heart's calling without any doubts about turning back. She followed her gut instinct, trusted her mission, and went on to achieve tremendous success. Admired for her immense talent, she's been in high demand for major acting roles ever since. Swank's journey was fueled by unwavering self-belief—she never gave up, no matter the challenges. She refused to see anyone as superior and knew that with dedication, anything was possible.

Imagine the struggles that propelled her forward—angst, depression, financial hardship, fierce competition, and the relentless discipline of mastering her craft. Yet, she always landed on her feet, turning real-life adversity into triumph. With confidence, passion, and devotion to her work, Swank exemplified grit and determination while staying true to her humble beginnings. Her success wasn't about shortcuts but relentless, focused motivation. While obstacles deter some, Swank's persistence defined her path. There are many ways to reach a goal—the key is finding the one that resonates with you. Her story is a testament to perseverance, resilience, and the power of unwavering belief.

Consider the challenges America faced in the 1950s and still faces today—racism, discrimination, and anti-Semitism. For many, these weren't just challenges but a living nightmare. In the Jim Crow South, extreme wealth disparity, murders, inequality, heartache, and pain permeated daily life, underscoring the prevalent unfairness. How did millions of people succeed and persevere through such adversity? How did they find the strength to endure these unimaginable hardships?

Perhaps you've experienced similar struggles firsthand or have studied history enough to understand the depth of their pain and disappointment. If you haven't faced these trials, consider yourself fortunate. For those who did, the price was immense. Despite these staggering difficulties, people found ways to endure through resilience, community support, unyielding hope, and determination. Their stories of perseverance are a testament to the strength of the human spirit. The feeling we get from supporting others and expressing our feelings is a shared experience that no monetary element can replace.

Today, a sense of imbalance and injustice remains across the globe. Struggles continue, echoing the challenges of the past. The world urgently needs compassion, peace, love, and understanding. Each of us can contribute something, no matter how small, to address these challenges. By fostering empathy, pushing for fairness, and encouraging social change, we can all help create a more just and compassionate world.

Simplify and focus on what truly matters to you. Navigating life's challenges requires determination and resilience in the face of distractions. Don't let the noise of the world steer you away from your own dreams. Avoid living a life based on others' expectations—your own aspirations are what matter most.

13
IMPLEMENT DAILY SUCCESS STRATEGIES

Consistency is vital for success. Establish daily habits and strategies to ensure continuous progress, focusing on the present moment and taking life one day at a time.

THIS CHAPTER COVERS:

Daily Strategies for Success
• Implement routines that support your goals.
• Resist falling back on excuses.
• Make small, consistent efforts towards your objectives.

Taking Life One Day at a Time
• Focus on the present and make the most of each day.
• Avoid getting overwhelmed by long-term plans and challenges.

DAILY STRATEGIES FOR SUCCESS

Implement Routines That Support Your Goals

A powerful daily strategy for success is establishing routines that support your goals. Creating a schedule and organizing your tasks lets you take control, making each day a step forward.

Engage with books that spark your curiosity or even consider writing one if the desire strikes. When you're busy testing out something new, it's amazing how progress feels fun and energizing. It gets you out of your head and allows your creativity to soar. A new version of yourself emerges. Whether leading an exercise group, starting a podcast or band, or joining an unexpected club, stay open-minded and watch the picture evolve. Once your discipline remains steady, you'll have cobbled together an immense collage of options and released deadwood.

When you start thriving in areas you previously considered uninteresting or trendy, you'll find yourself excelling at them. I've heard that of our 70,000 daily thoughts, 95 percent are retained and repeated the next day. To change your mind and surmount new frontiers we must be open to completely new horizons, or perhaps extreme directional change, rather than what has defined you.

Balance between the mental and the physical is the target, and when you hit that sweet spot, you'll know it. By staying active and alert, you'll keep stress at bay and be prepared for whatever challenges come next. Highly organized, prioritized, and disciplined—that's the new you, or perhaps the version of you that was always inside, just waiting to be unlocked. Once your physical body is healthy your spirit and imagination will excel equally.

The key now is to follow through, no matter what you're feeling or what challenges you're facing. Commitment is essential.

Without a structured schedule, it's easy to get lost. Complacency creeps in, and before you know it, hours are wasted and you're back in old, unproductive habits. Are you spending your afternoons in a coffee shop, chatting, while the world around you is making bold moves, chasing dreams, and bringing vivid imaginings to life? Taking breaks is important but living each day to the fullest means more than sitting around. You only get out what you put in—make sure you're making each moment count. Again: *Start.*

Resist Falling Back on Excuses

Those who are quick to make excuses often spend too much time second-guessing themselves and indulging in negative self-talk. Excuses and depression go hand-in-hand, sapping energy and motivation. To avoid feeling overwhelmed or confused, switch off these thoughts when they arise. Ask yourself, *are you truly responsible for anything, or do you constantly place blame elsewhere?*

Taking ownership of your actions, every day is an honest and healthy way to approach life. Excuses are simply a delay tactic or a cop-out—a way to avoid responsibility. In fact, they are a form of quitting—they signify giving up. Offering an excuse is a way of saying, "I've had enough. I'm done." If we become habitual excuse-makers, we start quitting on almost everything. Avoiding life's challenges makes things unnecessarily difficult. While you may legitimately feel exhausted, for those around you—like a spouse or boss—your excuses can be disheartening. Eventually, a boss might place an excuse-prone person in a corner cubicle, assigning tasks that match their avoidant personality. Over time, everyone grows tired of this behavior. Picture that person's desk cluttered with unfinished work—a direct reflection of their chaotic and disorderly mind, with disorganization and evasion of accountability running rampant.

On the flip side, this individual might resemble a well-meaning but absent-minded genius, interested in everything but unable to fulfill commitments. Despite their intelligence, excuses continue to pile up, schedules are neglected, and the train never leaves the station. The result is a cycle of potential never realized because of the habit of quitting.

Those who tend to make excuses often spend significant time and energy second-guessing themselves and engaging in self-doubt. The direction of our thoughts can either lead us toward greatness or plunge us into a state of dissatisfaction and stagnation, depending on how we manage them. Excuses and depression often stem from a lack of courage to examine our actions or challenge our beliefs. This can be fueled by fear-based anxieties or advice from unreliable sources.

It's crucial to evaluate the credibility of these sources—our own thoughts, beliefs, and even the philosophies passed down from our families—as they shape the way we perceive and approach the world.

Are you someone who takes responsibility for your outcomes, or do you tend to shift the blame onto others? Are you always the hero when things succeed, attributing success solely to your own efforts while disregarding the contributions of others?

Taking ownership of your actions, each day is an honest and healthy approach to life. It's not about seeking credit or assigning blame, as if life were a game of points. Regardless of whether you make every decision, the consequences—both positive and negative—are ultimately yours to bear.

Life presents us with countless decisions, and we have the privilege of making each one. Excuses are unproductive—supervisors appreciate hearing options and solutions from their teams, rather than unsolved problems. Becoming self-reliant, responsible, and focused cultivates confidence and builds character.

Along the way, you'll encounter remarkable individuals and develop compassion.

Excuses offer no escape. They often emerge from unchanging conditions and serve as a delay tactic or means of avoiding responsibility. Excuses can dampen others' spirits and lead to negative thought patterns, transforming us into pessimistic companions rather than positive, proactive individuals. Crafting excuses is time-consuming and can even lead to a web of lies to cover them up—a waste of time and energy. They don't serve anyone well and can bring the energy down in any room. Don't be the downer who spreads negativity!

Remember, excuses are a form of self-deception, a detrimental habit. You have control over your body and mind; take charge of how you think and respond. The words and actions of others never define you. Be discerning about what you believe; think critically; refrain from accepting unfounded assertions as truth. If negative influences drain your energy and nothing seems to go right, it's important to act and adjust. The situation won't change until you do.

If you once leaned on excuses, use humor to laugh at your old self. Shed that old version of you and aim to never be quick to anger or mean-spirited toward others. If you can laugh at yourself, especially in front of others, it's incredibly disarming, humbling, and refreshing.

Remain balanced—while we all want to be special, the truth is that we are all equal. Those who take themselves too seriously often lack humor and are prone to insecurity. When you're overly serious, you can become fragile, boring, or unnecessarily competitive.

Remember, competition often implies that you need to win, besting others in the process. But really, don't we want everyone to win? Isn't life about sharing love, equality, and compassion?

If it's all about you, you might end up alone, miserable, and unloved—a spot where no amount of money can fill the emptiness. Life is about giving love, and in turn, receiving it.

Make Small, Consistent Efforts Towards Your Objectives

Seize the day and celebrate each baby step along the way. Journal your thoughts, reflect on your progress, and always believe in yourself. Live a life with zero regrets and frequently double-check your direction to stay committed to your plan, adjusting as needed. Your ability to approach everything with a positive attitude, confidence, and poise will be your handshake to the world. It's not just preferable, it's essential to maintain a mindset focused on execution, paired with organized, deliberate actions to truly seize the day.

We can't force life, just as we can't force love. Some things must fall into place naturally for forward momentum to occur without external pressure. Don't rush—there's no need to exhaust yourself. Rushing often leads to chaos. Remain present and allow things to come to you, knowing that this takes patience. If you feel out of alignment, avoid making major decisions or changes. Often, the sweet spot is found in stillness and peace. Calm yourself and let the world flow through you like the ocean's waves or the breeze in the air.

If you find yourself constantly multitasking and struggling to bring things to completion, try organizing your workspace into sections. Create one area for tasks that must be addressed today, another for things to tackle tomorrow, and perhaps a third for items to discard or revisit later. If something has been lingering for far too long and isn't getting done, remove it from your space entirely and set a specific date to force yourself to address it. Alternatively, consider delegating the task if possible. Clear organization will help you regain focus and improve your productivity.

By focusing on incremental progress, especially when dealing with tasks you find difficult or have been avoiding, you create a sense of accomplishment without overwhelming yourself. Setting small, manageable goals each week allows room for creativity to flow and gently builds momentum without the risk of burnout. Rather than forcing every step, pacing yourself ensures that every action contributes to the larger picture. Small consistent efforts, especially in the face of procrastination, gradually turn into bigger strides toward success. This will prevent the kinds of roadblocks that often occur when expectations are pushed too quickly.

The "tortured genius" fascinates me—a brilliant yet deeply conflicted individual whose struggles often fuel creativity. This tension is common in music and art, where pain transforms into raw, compelling work. But there's a dark side. The same internal battles that drive artistry can lead to destructive behaviors, such as substance abuse, offering temporary relief but ultimately hindering growth. Understanding this dynamic means recognizing the fine line between brilliance and vulnerability. Some transcend their struggles, while others remain trapped in cycles of self-doubt and turmoil. Without self-awareness and balance, artists risk self-destruction, walking the thin line between profound expression and personal chaos.

The key to longevity and sustained creativity lies in maintaining a steady rhythm. Decisions made in a relaxed, composed state, not forced under pressure, tend to be the most effective. Like the old saying goes, "slow and steady wins the race."

TAKING LIFE ONE DAY AT A TIME

Focus on the Present and Make the Most of Each Day

The way we react to pressure and stress is a choice, and how we choose stems from our mindset and emotional resilience. It's easy to get caught up in negative emotions when facing unmet expectations or disappointments, especially when those expectations are tied to others. But how we handle those moments determines not only our well-being but also how others perceive and interact with us.

Indeed, discipline is a powerful force for your mind, guiding it towards consistent action. Remaining calm and composed, rather than allowing frustration to control us, often comes from developing emotional control and shifting our focus. Instead of placing heavy, unrealistic expectations on others or situations, a healthier approach is acceptance. Lowering your expectations will protect you from unnecessary frustration while also fostering better relationships through empathy and understanding. Living with gratitude and kindness helps you remain grounded.

This mindset of positive energy and acceptance invites more peace and love into your life, creating a cycle that benefits both you and others. It's true that life's challenges can feel overwhelming, especially as responsibilities pile up, but patience and active listening are tools that allow you to navigate them more gracefully. When you embrace this outlook, it becomes easier to face life's inevitable frustrations and setbacks without losing balance.

Paradoxically, a little preparation for the near future can help us focus on tomorrow when it comes. As mentioned earlier in this book, preparing the night before is a great strategy for ensuring a smoother, less stressful day ahead. By taking proactive steps like sketching diagrams, refining budgets, or reaching out for help in advance, you are setting yourself—and your team—up for success.

This foresight not only reduces stress but also allows for smoother collaboration. Each person knows their role, and everyone is working on separate fronts toward a shared goal, minimizing chaos. Are you running a business or a friendship? Define that conversation. If you're soft and friendly, colleagues will often view you that way and NOT get the job done. Decide!

The principle of **one day at a time** serves as a reminder to focus on today, staying present and maximizing each moment. It's about embracing the day and doing what you can to make it meaningful, whether you're tackling work or personal aspirations.

But it's also crucial to remember that life is short, and tomorrow isn't guaranteed. Integrating your dreams and bucket list into your daily life is essential. Take action toward your long-term desires now—don't wait until retirement to begin shaping your future and making your dreams a reality.

Avoid Getting Overwhelmed by Long-Term Plans and Challenges

Every day presents an opportunity to shape your reality. By deciding what will be productive, fun, or meaningful, you take control of the narrative. Dwelling on negativity—especially the things you can't control—drains bodily energy. What might seem like a painful setback or loss is just part of a larger process of learning.

Even future millionaires, successful business leaders, and top performers have faced numerous failures along their journeys. Failure is not personal; it's simply a lesson to learn and move past. Wins and losses are often relevant only to you. If you had seven wins and five losses yesterday, the victories are yours alone, even if no one else notices. Unsuccessful attempts are simply part of the trial-and-error process. No one is keeping score except you. Keep executing, trying out new ideas, and moving forward. With every step, you learn more and get closer to your goal.

When you run your own game, guided by a solid set of values, you'll often feel a rush of positive energy, like a runner crossing the finish line after a healthy lap. While the path can feel lonely at times, remember that as you stick to your mission and follow your own route, things will naturally fall into place. You're contributing your unique skills and talents to the world. Keep things simple and surround yourself with amazing people from whom you can learn. Share your knowledge to help make the world a better place. Mistakes are part of the process, and you'll never please everyone.

To manage feelings of overwhelm, pause and think carefully before taking action. Ask yourself:

- Why am I doing this? Do I truly love it and believe in it?

- Does it align with my goals and embody purpose, passion, and meaning?

- How does it impact others? Will it help or harm them?

- Is it ethical and the right thing to do for those affected?

- Is it beneficial for my community, or just for me?

- What will make me better than I was yesterday?

- Have I been complacent, lazy, or self-pitying lately?

Remember, you'll get out of life only what you put into it—nothing more. To be blunt, we each have to take responsibility for ourselves. No one can carry you forever; people have their own challenges and lives to live. No handouts. No shortcuts. It's up to you to step up.

This book has touched on many important topics with the aim of pushing you to think outside the box, to move beyond the comfort zone we often settle into. Thinking is hard work, but execution, action, and trying—this is where the true rewards lie. The main drivers are simple: START. TRY. RESET.

LET THINGS FLOW ...

I hope the ideas in this book have sparked inspiration, helping you to build confidence and explore exciting new paths that bring you immense joy. Whether trying a new sport, picking up a musical instrument, reading a novel, or visiting a new country—keep the challenges alive throughout your life. There's no age limit to growth and adventure.

Believe in yourself and let the confidence you build over time become your strength. Don't let fear, negativity, or the voices of others hold you back from moving forward. Grit is key to life. Hard work, not talk, is the foundation of progress. Happiness and fulfillment come from going outside of yourself and helping people, rather than inward, indulging in overthinking, ego, or narcissism.

Life is about experiences, not things. The journey is more important than your possessions, connections, or title. Instead of focusing on who you know, show us what YOU are doing. Be the kind of person you admire. You'll be remembered for how you make others feel, not what you own or your job title. Always remember that you never truly know the battles others are fighting, the struggles they keep hidden. Practice compassion and lead by example. Not everyone is as strong as you are.

Ultimately, we're all in this together; we need each other. Put aside differences and show respect for others' perspectives. Everyone cares about what they think and have to say. We all perceive the world differently, and none of us knows everything. Start each day with an open mind, humbly, as if you know very little—this makes life refreshing and exciting.

With every new endeavor, it's essential to invest in yourself. This is the true winning ticket. It brings progress, fulfillment, learning, and growth. Challenges will come, and with each one, you'll gain either wisdom or wounds. Complaining never solves anything. Instead, focus on finding solutions through research and personal experience. Your perspective, mindset, and reactions will shape your happiness. As noted, you create a powerful presence when you decide what you're going to react to. Silence, letting go, and compassion often work wonders.

Your mission must be designed by you and executed by you—there are no shortcuts. It's your life, and when you take full ownership of it, you'll make each day count. The journey requires effort, but the pride you'll feel when nothing was handed to you makes it all worthwhile.

I recently ran across these splendid words which distill so much of this book:

> *Life humbles you deeply. As the years pass, you start realizing how much time was wasted on nonsense, on meaningless arguments, on proving points, on chasing validation, and eventually you just stop. You stop forcing friendships, stop begging for love and stop seeking approval from those who never truly cared. You realize peace comes from within, not from the opinions of others. There's freedom in letting go. With age you understand that life isn't about material things, pride or ego. It's about your heart and who it beats for. You stop wanting more from the world and instead start wanting to experience it. The walls around your emotion begin to crumble and suddenly the simplest things feel beautifully poetic. A sunrise, a deep conversation, a moment of*

stillness, it all holds meaning. Because at the end of the day, true happiness isn't found in things; it's found in presence, peace, and the love you give freely.

Now go out there and power your life forward—do it for you. You'll be very glad you did!

CONCLUSION

Bold moves or nothing happens …

Much like a blank sheet of paper, the world is full of possibilities waiting for you to make the first stroke. You hold the power to make decisions—this will never change. Whether you choose to explore various paths, dive into things you're passionate about, or focus on specific details, the choices are yours. The goal is to embrace life fully, pursue your curiosity, and follow your dreams.

You have a great and huge life ahead of you, and now you are armed with a game plan that reflects your purpose—not that of others. Own your choices and your entire life. No, life isn't fair and never will be, but victimhood is a trap. Recognize your power in choosing how to respond and act. Don't waste energy trying to please everyone—doing so may steer you off track from your true purpose and rob you of life's joy. Instead, pursue what energizes you—with peace, love, joy, and enthusiasm—and do it with humility. Your positive karma is going to rotate the globe endlessly.

I've stressed the importance of attention to detail, for growth happens in the small moments, and when you simply TRY. Morning gratitude and meditative silence, telling someone you love them, looking into the sky breathing deeply, drinking hot tea with a splash of honey—do whatever naturally turns you on!

Life reveals itself in both triumphs and challenges. Through it all, never forget where you came from. Learn to forgive, take the high road, and don't waste time on negativity. Negative people are energy-draining—distance yourself from them. Life is fragile, and just a few bad decisions can create disaster. Remain vigilant, making each day count. The harder someone has it, the nicer I am to them. So much life may have been 100 percent out of their control. No judging!

Listen to everyone, regardless of their background—sometimes it's the unexpected people who offer the greatest wisdom. Remember, life's biggest lessons often come from failure, not success. When you encounter someone who doesn't resonate with you, observe, learn, and move on, carrying those golden insights with you. Compassion, insightfulness, and persistence are crucial in executing and following through on every little detail of your journey.

Your positive self-talk is your life's soundtrack—the melody that propels you forward. Refine it to reflect your beliefs, your passion, and your purpose. Make it a song that fuels your journey and keeps you aligned with your mission. Tomorrow is always a new opportunity to make strides.

Share your knowledge generously and make helping others a priority whenever possible. The energy you invest in uplifting others inevitably reflects, multiplying the impact of your journey. For me, the journey began in the world of architects, engineers, and craftsmen in custom building, later transitioning to music production as an artist.

It's in this artistic realm that I internalized many of the principles outlined in this book. I had the esteemed privilege of collaborating with world-renowned recording engineers and producers, including two records with a huge legend in the late recording engineer Steve Albini of Chicago's Electrical Audio. Indeed a one-of-a-kind genius on any given level.

Steve, who famously declined the title of producer, is often celebrated as the greatest recording engineer of all time. Over an extraordinary career he engineered over 3,500 records, crafting music for icons like Nirvana-Kurt Cobain, Paul McCartney, and Led Zeppelin. Tragically, Steve Albini passed away during the writing of this book, May 2024. On my next recording with Jason Narducy, walking past Steve's chair, console, and meticulously designed studio, was a stark wake-up call—a reminder that all this joy and creativity could end tomorrow.

Learning from true artists who led by example and poured their hearts into their craft taught me innumerable lessons. Witnessing Steve's laser-focused dedication—his eyes closed in deep concentration as he leaned back during playbacks—was to witness perfectionism in motion. He embodied purpose, passion, and ethics; always putting the artist first, treating every person and record equally, famously refusing royalties, and maintaining a grand yet humble presence in an enormous industry. Albini often answered the phone, even when I called several times, thoroughly answering questions no matter who called. A college student's concerns about an internship equaled those of world famous rockstars. My 100 hours there was like a dream I often reflect upon.

Another legendary beacon of artistry was multi-instrumentalist producer Alan Weatherhead; His immense talent taught me daily lessons in humility amidst a low-key chill presence, never taking himself too seriously. Al's musical talents are in the same realm as Bob Dylan's, yet he's an understated rockstar who brings zero attention to himself. His contributions were invaluable to seven of my records. Virginia had the luxury of this Wisconsin native's endless gifts and expertise.

The more I immersed myself in the disciplines of music and production, observing the focus and discipline of these brilliant individuals, the more I discovered depth, inspiration, and a never-quit attitude. They weren't just people who won the day for themselves—they made dreams come true for thousands of struggling artists. You could see it in their demeanor, daily conduct, but especially in their eyes: a quality so profound you wish it could be replicated for the entire human race. We can all learn from these creative souls, and I wish you the opportunity to encounter equally wonderful people in your own life.

As you follow your dreams, be magnanimous in all things and take good care of our planet. Always be the bigger person. Do the right thing and tell yourself the truth. Lying to yourself is a complete waste of the limited time you have. Don't forget the man who said, "I never had a bad day." Even if it isn't always true for me, I just love saying his words. Ha!

Lastly, always go front and center, knowing that old adage: If you don't believe in yourself, nobody else can. When you try, then fail, then try again, confidence is built, and you get to own it forever!

Thank you for taking the time to read through these thoughts. You have no idea how much it means to me, and I hope you felt big energy and love drifting your way from Virginia's Blue Ridge Mountains! After writing and performing on thirteen albums and traveling to fifty countries, I saw writing this book as an opportunity to explore a different writing style—sharing real-life experiences and principles that I hope spark new ideas or help you in some small way.

If you have time, please check out my music under my name, available on platforms like Spotify, SoundCloud, iTunes, Bandcamp, YouTube, and Amazon. My songs range from alternative rock to love ballads, and sometimes folk tunes.

Again, thank you! All the best to you.

Stephen Jacques

A FINAL THOUGHT

Taking full responsibility for your life is essential.

No one is coming to rescue you from the realities of life—no cavalry, no miracle. The sooner you accept this truth and step into leadership over every area of your life, the smoother your journey will become.

In childhood, we often have the support of family, guidance from teachers, and moments that help us build confidence. But as we grow, disappointments can mount if we ignore important details, reject wise counsel, or allow arrogance and stubbornness to take root.

Progress doesn't come from rushing. It comes from moving deliberately—slowly, methodically, and with precision. That's where you'll find stability, peace, harmony, and a sense of control. It's not unlike preparing for a journey through river rapids: the ride may be rough and unpredictable, but with careful preparation, you can navigate it with strength and clarity.

Stephen Jacques

ACKNOWLEDGMENTS

In life, we come to deeply appreciate the support and friendship of those who truly listen—those who are present and attuned, always making things better.

A heartfelt thank you to my exceptional editors: Amy Touchette, who undertook the enormous task of shaping this, my first book, distilling twenty-three chapters down to a purposeful thirteen. Her effort made it possible for this work to truly take form. And to Pat Dobie, who came in during the final stages to polish and refine it with her masterful touch. Amy and Pat bring decades of experience and an intuitive understanding of the written word. Their editorial guidance brought clarity, rhythm, and balance—like steadying a pottery wheel until the piece spins true. Amy, based in New York City, is a respected editor, photographer, teacher, and mentor. Pat, in Vancouver, is equally admired for her writing, teaching, and editing expertise. You are both more appreciated than you'll ever know.

Chris Scardina performed the layout and typesetting for the print versions of the book, along with uploading to the printer and coordinating with others such as cover artist Emma Johnson; I thank you both.

I am profoundly grateful to Professor Scott Hudson for his ongoing advice and support of both this book and my music.

ABOUT THE AUTHOR

Stephen R. Jacques earned his B.S. in Mechanical Engineering and is world-renowned as an accomplished musician, having released thirteen albums—including two highly successful collaborations with legendary producer Steve Albini (Nirvana, Paul McCartney). With 40 years of professional work experience, his career spans extensive world travel, managing high-end building projects, hiring architects, navigating complex contract negotiations, and contributing to both corporate and university environments. His journey has also included acting in Hollywood, creating a local TV show, mentoring students, and engaging in numerous benevolent endeavors. A self-made renaissance man and true professional, Stephen put himself through college, launched his own business, and has consistently given back—helping the homeless, supporting those living below the poverty line, and providing aid in the aftermath of natural disasters. If there is anyone who has truly 'walked the walk' it is Stephen. Broken8 Records Australia published these words: "Stephen Jacques is arguably one of the most expressive and understated artists of his generation."

www.ingramcontent.com/pod-product-compliance
Lightning Source LLC
Chambersburg PA
CBHW070850050426
42453CB00012B/2122